MW01289900

A Six-Pack of Hitchhiking Stories

KENNY FLANNERY

Kenny Flannery

Copyright © 2019 Kenny Flannery
All rights reserved.

Contact: HoboLifestyle@gmail.com

Cover photo and editing by: Julie Butler

ISBN: 978-1-07-269015-3

A Six-Pack of Hitchhiking Stories

For my uncle, Ken Butler.

"It is what it is."

CONTENTS

Pre-game

In 2007, I left a "stable" life in New York City. Taking only what I could carry, I set off across the United States, and the world. After more than a decade, I'm still going.

Hitchhiking proved to be an effective means of transport, but also an enlightening window into other people's lives. Often, as you'll see, a ride becomes much more than getting from A to B.

Beer is amazing. You already knew that. I've drank to the extremes of quality and quantity while rambling the globe. From brewing to drinking, beer has weaved its way through my travels on all levels.

These six stories will give you a peek into my nomadic lifestyle. They'll also explain things I never dreamed of, like going to Beer Camp and becoming a minor celebrity in Ireland by drinking lots of beer.

Crack open each chapter and experience the aromas of freedom and tastes of adventure. Get drunk off the road's intoxicating allure that seduced me into a life of endless travel. Sip it slow or chug away. Cheers to beers, and here's to the good times.

Suggested drinking

Don't just read. Drink!

This book is best read by pairing each chapter with an appropriate beer. Some are obvious and easily found. Others, like Ryeway 117, no longer exist. You'll have to get creative. Use what you've got, but here's some guidance:

American Amber: Any sessionable beer will do, but New Belgium Fat Tire is recommended.

German Schwarzbier: Get your hands on a dark lager.

Belgian Quad: Are you gonna hitchhike to the abbey like I did? No? Then look for St. Bernardus Abt 12 in any respectable bottle shop.

Northwestern IPA: Drink what I drank while searching for the hidden keg: a Northwestern style IPA. Bonus if you get the beer I helped bottle: 10 Barrel Apocalypse IPA.

Ryeway 117: You missed it! Sierra Nevada's Ruthless Rye will work in a pinch.

Irish Stout: Guinness. Or the best stout available.

AMERICAN
AMBER

"It's gonna work *too* well," I pleaded with a smile. "Really, though, I don't wanna fool people."

Even still, she stayed, beaming her bubbly, too-perfect smile at the oncoming traffic. Her thumb extended out towards them with confident excitement as she playfully ignored me.

I met Camille just five months earlier. She was a soft-glow kind of pretty — a blonde-haired, light-eyed, ex-Mormon turned semi-hippie. Together we looked like a non-threatening, carefree couple on a fringe adventure; there was no doubt someone would stop.

They did in no time. I snatched up my backpack and said my goodbye's to her as I ran up towards the white pickup truck. Sure enough, though, they noticed it was just me coming for them, without the bubbly, smiling girl. They peeled back out into traffic before I even got close.

"Yup," I sighed, turning back, "That's what I'm talking about."

"OK, OK," she said, still beaming.

She hung around another minute finishing her cigarette, dreaming in the final hesitation before lifting her bike from the grass. She shot me grinning look-back's and grand waves as she pedaled away, leaving me to face the road on my own.

I was as relieved as I was disenchanted to see her disappear into the Salt Lake City side streets. For a few moments I daydreamed about her getting out of Utah and joining me on my indefinite ramblings, down to South America like we'd been fruitlessly musing about for months. How easy, free and light it would be.

I snapped out of it, and returned to the task at hand. I raised my cardboard "Denver" sign in one hand and held out my thumb in the other. Laramie was my first stop on the way — all part of a scheme that got dreamt up the night before.

Camille's housemate, Carl, was going to a soccer game in Denver with talk of brewery hopping. Two more friends were in my ear about a "bicycle bar crawl" in Laramie. The timing lined up and, as usual, I was open and willing for whatever good idea came about.

Denver was where I'd first been exposed to homebrewing. I was staying with someone whose roommate was busy with it in the kitchen, happy to tell me all about it as I helped. I'd already been getting into craft beer before that, but the encounter propelled my interest even further.

With Colorado and all it's great beer in mind I locked my eyes on the bumper of a single oncoming car. It felt like I used some Jedi, gravitational mindtrick as he eased to a stop in the shoulder ahead of me. I hopped in and met the old ski bum heading towards some land he owned near Park City.

"Usually I don't pick up hitchhikers," he started after we'd settled in, a typical line. "The last guy I picked up just kept rambling and rambling and rambling and mumbling through all of it. I couldn't understand a word — and he stunk! I ended up pulling off at the first truck stop I saw and told him it was as far as I was going."

After he turned, I walked alongside the highway until a car pulled halfway over into the shoulder. I ran up and got in before someone would honk or even smash into him. About my age, in his mid-twenties, the stony driver was wearing a necklace with orange beads and a glass mushroom hanging in the center. He was only going across town, but I was glad to be maintaining my momentum. The day was warm and breezy with a few clouds in the sky amidst the mountains; I didn't mind the waits between rides.

A middle-aged woman in a pickup truck stopped for me next.

"You looked clean-cut, so that's why I stopped," she admitted.

I got that line a lot too, with or without my beard. She gabbed on about how she just got fired from her job at the IRS and how inefficient it was. Ranting on, she became increasingly animated about her hatred for her bosses. Soon she was shouting in the car just as loud as she had shouted at them when they took her into their office to fire her.

"I slid *one* badge across the table, '*You can shove this one up your ass!*' Then slid my *other* security card to my *other* boss and said, 'And you can shove *this* one up *your* ass!' and then I walked out of the office. Everyone could hear me," she asserted smugly.

She turned off onto Interstate 84, leaving me moseying forward as I munched on a granola bar, and ignoring traffic for a moment.

Despite my daze, a car faded over to the roadside ahead of me.

Bloop! Bloop!

I looked back mid-run to see a police car blasting its siren past me. The car I'd thought was stopping for me was instead getting pulled over.

I slowed to a casual pace. As I passed the car, the cop was already standing by the driver's window, questioning him about speeding or whatever it may have been. I crept right on by, gesturing to the cop with a subtle nod — a calculated sign of uninterested politeness. He did the same. I've dealt with cops a lot while hitchhiking and knew better than to engage unnecessarily. Although the results are often harmless (and even helpful at times), it's best to leave it alone.

Despite the scene, I started walking backwards with my thumb out facing the traffic. Someone stopped right away. I ran for it as I imagined the scene from the perspective of others driving by: a backpacked lunatic running full-speed from a cop car towards his getaway vehicle.

This driver was a year or two younger than myself with bushy brown hair and squinty, red eyes. After a few miles of distance from the cop he rolled a confirming spliff as we got to talking. His car was packed with most of his belongings; he bounced between living in Washington state and Boulder where he'd be heading after a stint in Steamboat Springs.

We hit his turnoff and before long I was jumping into the backseat of a pickup truck that stopped for me. The consistent flow of rides continued.

The guy in the passenger seat didn't speak while the driver did nothing but. This self-proclaimed hillbilly had a story about seeing a covered wagon wheeling on past his house.

"I had to get to the bottom of that!" he said with passion. "There was a woman with her son who'd started in Nevada on their way to Texas at a rate of twelve to twenty miles a day, retracing what her grandfather had done back in the day."

The hillbilly was overjoyed as he recounted the details of this interaction. That story was about all he had time for before our roads split, leaving me under the gray Wyoming skies. I walked optimistically forward and, sure enough, an eighteen-wheeler yielded to my thumb.

"Laramie for sure!" I shouted to myself as I sprinted the hundred yards it had taken them to brake. He was walking around the side of the truck by the time I got up to him.

"This may be a stupid question to ask, but are you honest?" he cautiously asked.

"Yes indeed!" was the thing to say. He opened the door and I climbed up in.

"You looked OK, but you never know," he said. "I usually don't pick people up."

He was a year younger than me, but had been trucking ever since he was tall enough to reach the pedals. He took a lot of pride in his rig, everything inside was clean and chromed out. The truck's logo was tattooed on his arm.

"I told you I love Peterbilt!" he grinned.

He said he saw a hitchhiker almost every day. In the two years I'd been hitching around the country I usually heard the opposite.

"I'll never, ever pick up a girl though," he asserted. "My friend picked one up that seemed OK, but when he got to the next truck stop, there were police waiting — she called them trying to blackmail him! She was going off about how he'd tried to take advantage of her, this and that," he sighed in frustrated disgust.

"Turns out she had a record of doing this kind of thing, so nothing happened to him," he said. "They told him to drive off and they'd deal with the bitch. I don't even wanna mess with that."

He was headed all the way to New Jersey along I-80. The thought of riding along such a distance tempted me — the whole of America and all its potential was ahead of us.

But Laramie was the scene for now, I reaffirmed. I'd have to let the eastbound miles drift on without me. Instead, I stuck to the idea at hand, hopping out into the small city as it cropped up in the darkness off the highway.

Zak and Anthony arrived the next day, decked out in MC Hammer pants, goggles, capes and goofy attire they'd gotten at a thrift store. They'd found us a place to stay with a guy named Maxim who I linked up with when I arrived. Now he was stepping out of his bedroom looking caped and goggled the same as them, with bandanas tied all over himself.

"Tour de Laramie!" he announced joyously. "So it begins!"

Once a year people biked through the streets with the goal of having a drink at every bar in the city — there were twenty-eight to visit this year.

This was an easy sell and the reason I was here. I dug a bowtie out of my backpack that I'd been needlessly carrying around since a friend's wedding; now was the time for it. It matched imperfectly perfect with the faded American flag colored cape Maxim handed off to me in the shuffle.

Six of us hopped on bikes they'd scrambled together. The first bar was right around the corner. We burst in, marched directly to the bar and proudly held up shots of tequila.

"Gentlemen," Maxim proclaimed. "To the Tour de Laramie!"

We slammed them down and went right back out the door to the bikes. We continued in this fashion, lingering longer if the bar's cheapest drink was a full beer or the crowd held our attention.

Some bars were ready for those of us on tour with jello shots or cheap watered down shots for a dollar. There were good beers, crap beers, hefty shots, and sweet shots; dive bars, hotel bars, sports bars, and chain restaurants — we ran the gamut. Other ragtag groups of cyclists crossed our path or joined us. One mob of twenty odd people wore matching concert-like T-shirts with all the bars in town listed on the back.

We heedlessly careened down the Laramie streets in a swarm as cars honked and cheered us on — at least that's how we perceived it.

We hazily binged on, one to the next. Even the bowling alley had a bar where we stopped and played a few frames. Someone had the presence of mind to guide us back to Maxim's place for an impromptu backyard-barbecue to fuel up on something other than booze, but then it was right back out into the madness.

Late into the night, I found myself without anyone I'd started with. I'd gotten caught up flirting with a girl from another group and soon that gang had dispersed as well.

I stumbled out to the sidewalk and found my

bike in the jumble of others out front. Suddenly, I recalled where my newfound friends had left for: home.

I had an idea of what the address was, but no idea where I was in relation to anything tangible. Hoping to get on track, I pedaled around asking for directions, and occasionally getting sidetracked with other drunks holding onto the night.

I wheeled over a bridge knowing this was either very good or very much the wrong direction. When I saw a cop car coming, I decided it was time for a bold move. I swerved into his lane and halted with my hand out, pulling *him* over for a change.

He was good-humored, at first. I gave him my hazy recollection of Maxim's address and he somehow pointed me in the right direction. His demeanor changed once he'd gotten the needed information across.

"If I see you on that bike again you'll be in the jail for the night," he warned.

"Alrighty," I complied, trying to diffuse any conflict. "Thanks!"

It hadn't occurred to me until then that one could get a DUI on a bicycle. I walked the bike down the street until he was out of sight and then saddled back on, bursting through the chilly air into the side streets. I was too drunk, passionate and impatient to obey his authoritative request.

The precise path to Maxim's still wasn't clear, but as I felt I was getting closer, I asked a guy on the sidewalk for directions.

"Oh man, I'm not even from here," he replied.

"My friend would probably know, though," he told me. "She's just a block up. That's where I'm heading now."

We jabbered back and forth as I told him about the great Tour until we got to the house.

"She's probably sleeping," he said. "I'll wake her up, though; it's all good."

"You sure?" I laughed, asking for confirmation that was already implied.

"Yeah, man, it's cool," he said as he pushed the bedroom door open.

"Wake up Kelly, we've got a visitor all the way from New York City!"

"Ah…," she yawned awake. "You fuckers."

She surrendered to the situation, having apparently just laid down after a long night of drinking herself.

"Directions! Directions!" my new friend cried. "Where's this guy gotta go?"

"Back to New York!" she quipped.

He bounced on the bed with his knees like a child on a trampoline, pestering her awake.

"Where are all my friends?" I demanded answers without any kind of straight face. "Where did you hide them?"

"I'm your only friend, you know that!" she tittered. "Lay down and shut your pretty face down."

Before long the guy had left us alone in the room, and I was indeed laying down with her. She was scratching my chest and I'd somehow started massaging her neck as I tried to coax directions out of her.

"That feels really good," she whispered fadingly.

I could have fallen into the night right there, but I was on a mission. As drunk as I was I still had in mind that Maxim and the others would be scattering out of town in the morning — my backpack would be locked away indefinitely.

I kept the girl talking and eventually pulled useful directions out of her. I eased out of the bed like a parent sneaking away from a child, tucked her in and shut the door behind me.

"So that's Kelly," her friend said, smirking at me from the kitchen as I came out. "You know where you're going?"

"Yeah, I think so," I grinned dumbly back.

"Well, have a shot on your way out!"

He was already pouring a couple.

I hopped on the bike one last time and sure enough, she'd steered me right. The sight of the house was a relief. I quietly slipped in the door and despite the sprawl of passed out bodies, there was still one unoccupied couch to fall onto. Success.

I slowly came to in the morning. As sunlight streamed in a few people started stirring as well.

"You're here!" Zak remarked, still from the comfort of his sleeping bag. "What happened to you last night?"

I told him what I remembered. While recalling the story of pedaling around the cold, I realized that

I left all my warm gear at the last bar. My long-sleeved shirt, sweatshirt, rain jacket, hat, gloves — all gone. My liquid sweater had been substantial, apparently.

The front door burst open as we still laid there. A guy I recognized from the night before — Keith — walked in, and looked right at me.

"I'll be back in twenty minutes," he said. "Will you be good to go?"

"Yeah, yeah, for sure," I affirmed blindly. He turned back outside letting the door close behind him.

"Where are you guys going?" Zak verbalized the question I was already pondering. Somehow hearing him ask it jolted my memory.

"The breweries!" I answered to both of us.

Somewhere in the thick of the night I'd brought up how I'd be hitching to Denver next to see my friend and visit some breweries. Being a beer lover himself, he'd offered to drive down with me to hit some spots on the way.

Twenty minutes later he was back from prying his hungover friend Matt out of bed and into the car to join us. They also remembered the last bar we'd been at together. We dropped in and, miraculously, they had the whole bundle of my forgotten warmth in a pile waiting for me.

With that, we headed towards Colorado. Our first stop was New Belgium Brewery in Fort Collins. We were too late for the tour, but anyone who walked in could choose four substantial samples of whatever they wanted. The hungover Matt lethargically abstained from his seat at the table, but Keith and I each enjoyed a well-crafted helping of hair-of-the-dog.

A little further down the road we reached Left Hand Brewery in Longmont. This time Matt didn't join us at all. Not only did he have no interest in drinking, he had no interest in even leaving the car. Keith and I checked in for pints of their famed Milk Stout, then were quickly back out on the road heading towards Boulder.

On the way, we realized the particular brewery we wanted to visit next was closed on this day. Between that and Matt's continued moans of dissent, turning back to Laramie was imminent. Keith expressed some genuine apprehension about not taking me clear to Denver, as we'd (drunkenly) discussed, but I swiftly put him at ease. Hitchhiking had been my plan all along, I assured him. Not only that, but they were leaving me near a bustling gas station only sixty miles north of the city.

I thumbed a ride in a matter of minutes — the SUV blasting 90s hip-hop had me hopping out in downtown in less than an hour.

I called my friend Carl straight away, but as the phone rang my meager reality began to sink in. The carefree bar hopping in Laramie had drained my feeble pockets. Carl was with a big crew going from bar to bar and stretching my last dollars ranged between tricky and impossible. He sensed my trepidation on the phone.

"I'll sponsor you, man, you actually made it!" he assured me. "We'll get you into the game, too."

The casual nature of his genuine generosity put me at ease.

I found him a dozen blocks away at a brewery with the other already drunk soccer fans, some of which I recognized from Salt Lake. Within moments I had a mug full of a stout in front of me and blended right in. This was the third or fourth brewery they'd been to so far. We stepped over to Great Divide after for another round before piling into a van headed to the stadium.

After tailgating in the light rain we pushed inside to the stands. People in our crew brought drums, flags and everything — all exceptionally rowdy as we cheered on the visiting Real Salt Lake team. I hadn't been a fan or even known about the team until just hours ago, but I was screaming all the same with the rest of them. Little kids and grown men alike cursed at us as we relentlessly heckled their local team. In the end they got the best of us, though, as we lost 2 to 0.

As we filed out a girl who'd been next to us in the stands bumped into me playfully.

"Where's the after-party?" she smiled.

"I'm sure we'll find out shortly," I buzzed.

She put her number in my phone and I headed back to the hotel with Carl and the others. We got some food in us and were ready to get back to it, but everyone else was partied out. I gave the girl a call, then met her at a nearby brewhouse with her friends for several rounds of beers. They insisted on sprinkling in shots of Jägermeister — the main reason for the haze to follow.

A blast of morning light woke me up as the curtains slid open. Carl was shuffling out of the hotel room with a couple of the girls while another was laying next to me.

"See you later, man," he stammered as he exited.

My backpack was tucked in the corner of the room reassuringly — always a pertinent check to make when waking up in such conditions. I hazily recalled grabbing it from his room before coming to this one. I vaguely remembered drinking on the balcony and carrying on, but the specifics weren't as clear.

"Where's he heading?" I asked the girl next to me.

"They're taking him back to his hotel," she said sleepily as she stood up. "We'll meet them downstairs and get going in fifteen or twenty minutes."

I got up and moving as memories dazed back in, slowly. I grabbed my pack and an armful of their stuff and brought it down to the lobby where they were waiting. We piled into their SUV where I was relegated to the way back with the luggage. The actual seats were full with the four girls and one teenager I gathered was one of their daughters. I was still unclear what I'd gotten into as we rolled out of downtown.

"So uh... where to today?" I asked purposely broadly, although not well disguised.

"Let's get breakfast first!" one girl petitioned, either ignoring me or misunderstanding. I stayed quiet, listening for clues as we turned into a drive-thru. Soon after we were rolling up onto the freeway.

"So how long is the drive anyhow?" I asked again, trying to glean some useful information.

"Um… I think it's about seven or eight hours to Ogden, but probably just seven to where you'll wanna be dropped off," she said. "The highways change directions pretty close to Salt Lake."

Salt Lake City; everything came together. In the drunken night they must've mentioned they were heading to Ogden and had room in the car. With an open agenda, and incitement from Carl, I apparently jumped on the free ride opportunity. I closed my eyes and tried to recapture some sleep, already contemplating my escape — again — from Salt Lake. Drunk me thought it was a good idea, but my hungover self was over the scene in that city, for the time-being at least.

From where they dropped me off I hitched just one ride from a guy heading right into the city and he went out of his way to drop me at Carl and Camille's house. I walked in and they were both in the kitchen. Camille sighed with a smirk and Carl gave a knowing nod to the previous night.

"I got a plane ticket and *flew* back here, and you roll in just a half an hour after me — hitchhiking," he laughed. "Only Kenny, man."

I laughed.

"Yeah, man, but I rode in the trunk with those crazy girls until Ogden, practically," I said. "I was so confused."

I pulled out a cheap plastic bottle of vodka from my backpack.

"They gave me this on the way out for whatever reason," I said.

I stuck it in the freezer where it would reportedly remain untouched for months.

"The last ride I got was from some guy who was neighbors with Mrs. Fields up in the mountains — the cookie lady or whatever — talking about how she's got a place with twenty-seven bedrooms," I explained.

"He says she tried to bully him into going halfsies on a firetruck or something," I smiled and sighed.

"Well," I paused. "I guess I'll head south tomorrow... Vegas, Phoenix," I pondered. "Onto the next thing."

GERMAN
SCHWARZBIER

I grew up with the generational perspective that Germany was an epic beer country. While it's true it has a deep brewing history and that most German beer is not technically terrible, these days the country wouldn't even scratch a top-ten list.

Any objective craft beer drinker (disregarding history or nostalgia) would much rather be planted on a bar stool in Brussels, Copenhagen or nearly any surrounding country. Germany was left behind while the rest of the world explored new tastes, textures and flavor extremes.

"Reinheitsgebot!" a sympathizer may argue back. They'll be citing the German purity law that states beer can only be made with barley, hops, water (and yeast),

"Germany stays true to these original ingredients — that's why it hasn't evolved," they exclaim.

This silly argument doesn't explain Germany's lack of world-class IPAs, stouts and other ales that push the limits of flavor without straying from these simple core ingredients either.

What Germany lacks in innovation, they make up for in volume, atmosphere and an embraced culture of day-drinking. You could start by pointing at the prominence of beer gardens and extend that to the parks and riverfronts filled with beer drinkers simply enjoying the outdoors.

Even though they lack a dynamic range in style, the range they do have is made with prideful precision. The country isn't sloshing down the likes of Bud Light when it's time to kick back. I was more than willing to dive in.

My first trip into Berlin was brief. I'd hitchhiked there from Amsterdam and stayed only for a night to touch base with George, a traveler I'd met the previous summer in California. He and his friend Luis, who lived in Berlin, were flying to a wedding in Romania. They invited me to join, saying it would be a hell of a party and the bride wouldn't mind at all.

Without the luxury of a plane ticket, I hitched my way there over several days before enjoying the weekend of festivities. Since I was already that far east I decided to keep going, hitching on to Istanbul to see my friend Warren who was living there temporarily.

We'd met up in Alaska a few summers back and hitched down the long way to Vancouver together. Like me, he'd been living out of his backpack for years except he'd "settle down" every so often in a new place to focus on a tech company he'd started.

Istanbul got the best of him, however. While hitchhiking into Turkey he got dropped off at the Greek border where the guard presented him with a problem. He said he could stamp him out of Greece, but he wouldn't be allowed to cross into Turkey on foot. A tour van pulled up behind and the driver overheard the dilemma. Despite subtle complaints from her passengers she offered to let Warren (a massively tall Dutch hitchhiker with heavy metal hair past his shoulders) ride the minor couple-minutes drive to the Turkish side.

While Warren's and the passengers passports got stamped he shared his story with the van driver, mentioning he'd be looking for a room to rent in Istanbul. They wound up exchanging numbers, as it turned out there could possibly be a room in her apartment available.

He got a ride himself shortly after from a friendly guy heading straight to Istanbul. They arrived at dark, but the guy who gave him a ride had a spare room and offered it up for the night. One night turned into months — they got along well and Warren offered to start paying him rent.

Even though he now had a room, he couldn't ignore the phone number of the pretty van driver from the border. He made the call. In time they'd get married, move back to the Netherlands and have a kid together.

When I arrived, they were still only a few weeks removed from that initial phone call — they'd just started dating. I enjoyed Istanbul and hanging out with my good friend, but the beer is even worse than in Germany. And to be fair, at that time I was still under the ruse that German beer was legit. I was thirsty to return.

Berlin, in particular, was calling my name. I turned right on around, hitching my way back pausing only a couple days each in Vienna, Brno and Prague. At the outskirts of the museum-like Czech city I had one last pilsner before throwing my thumb out.

I was encouraged as I started getting rides right away, albeit short ones at first. After several of these little jumps I was dropped off at a gas station where a couple other hitchhikers were waiting for a lift themselves.

Rather than waiting for them to catch a ride, I opted to walk past them and straight onto the motorway itself. This isn't always legal, and other hitchhikers will argue that cars are going too fast, but this often works out well for me. This time was no exception.

Within minutes I got a ride from three German girls in their early twenties coming from a camping trip in Bulgaria. They were all irrefutably beautiful, glowingly effervescent as they reflected on their vacation. That energy was sustaining as they looked giddily ahead to their friend's week-end birthday celebration in Berlin. We gassed on up forward, chattering back and forth in the collective spirit of the road.

Traffic came to a standstill as we neared the city. They seized the moment to hop out of the car, rummaging through backpacks to change into party clothes. Suddenly, traffic started moving and they giggled uncontrollably as Karin scrambled back to the driver seat with her bra only halfway on. The others touched up their faces with makeup, feeling whimsical with the frantic pace they'd created.

"You should come!" they offered as we inched forward.

"It's out in the country at his parent's farmhouse, everyone is gonna be camping for the weekend," the girl sitting next to me said. "There's gonna be bands playing, an open bar all weekend, plenty of food..."

"I think they're doing a pig roast!" Karin chimed in.

"They are!" another cried excitedly. "I think he's asking people to chip in three or four euros or something for the whole weekend; it's basically free. You should come!"

Some of life's choices are too easy.

We arrived and were handed beers straight away, bratwurst, too. A bonfire was blazing and the night was igniting. I whirled around listening to most everyone speak in German, sipping the malty schwarzbier at hand. Nearly everyone spoke English as well, even if I was the only one who benefited.

They all got a kick out of the way I'd stumbled into this situation — from the side of the road to the place to be.

Sliding out of my sleeping bag and into a mug of coffee, the next day began. Sweet rolls and other treats were laid out. I grazed for a while, then helped move some boxes and set up the bar for the coming night. A giant pig was prepped and being roasted, just as the girls had mentioned.

By late morning the beers started popping open. Soon after shots were poured from strange un-marked bottles. Bugs were crawling around on a projector aimed at the wall and loads more people were spilling in by late afternoon.

By the time the music was in full force I realized I was, too. The dark schwarzbier had been going down like breaths of air. A couple German guys had taught me a phrase that sounded something like "Das geil!" They told me it meant: "Fucking amaz-ing!" I remember they had me shouting it up at the band in the barn as they smiled and played harder. Laughter, smiles and dancing in every direction. The bonfire was raging again next to the barn. Circ-ling that fire is the last thing I remembered.

I gradually opened my eyes to afternoon light spilling over me. As I became conscious of my un-familiar surroundings — on a couch in a bright liv-ing room — I remembered the bonfire. Then Berlin, the barn, the party and the girls who'd brought me there. I was supposed to have woken up in my sleeping bag in the field behind that barn. My urge to fall back asleep battled my sense of urgent curiosity.

An unfamiliar face appeared in the hallway, blankly glancing at me as they stepped into a bathroom. Scanning the room I hoped to spot my backpack or any kind of clue as to where I was. I'd blacked out before in my days of drinking, but this was completely dark. Beyond the bonfire I remembered nothing and was in a totally different environment now. It wasn't clear I was still in Germany even. Most disconcerting was the absence of my pack.

Finally, someone recognizable appeared — the guy from the party who'd had me shouting "Das geil!" He smiled as he sat down at the desk next to me. Before I could say a word I saw a girl walk past the door in the hallway too, one of the three who'd picked me up. I began talking with the guy next to me, hoping some more clues would spill out, something to jog my memory. I pulled myself off the couch to join him in the kitchen when he suggested coffee.

Clues weren't coming fast enough, and I was past trying to conceal the fact that I'd completely blacked out. At last I had to just ask him what the hell happened.

"Do you remember 'Das geil'?" he chuckled. "You kept shouting that at the band and all around. Every time I saw you you had the biggest smile on your face, telling jokes and cracking everyone up. Do you remember jumping over the fire?"

"Not at all, but that sounds about right," I offered. "Did I fuck myself up?"

I became aware of my body for the first time since I'd gotten up. I didn't feel any burns or bruises.

"No, a few of you were all jumping over it, it was crazy!" he continued. "You were flirting with all the girls."

"You and Lena were making out for a while," he laughed. "You guys thought you were hidden, but you were only twenty meters from the fire!"

"Who's Lena?" I asked curiously.

"Lena — she's the one who gave you the ride, the blonde girl who drove you."

"Ah, right, right," I said. "Where is she? Does she live here too?"

"No, she lives in the suburbs," he explained. "When it started to rain we all decided to come back home instead of camping again."

He laughed loudly again as he recalled more.

"You took a pie when we left and were offering slices to everyone on the train and on the street," he said. "People thought you were crazy."

"Did anyone take a slice?" I grinned, knowing this sounded like something I'd do.

"Yes!" he chortled, "But most people thought you were crazy!"

"Do you have any idea where my backpack is — did I bring it back?" I suddenly remembered the more pressing matter.

"Lena has it, she packed that and your sleeping bag in her car," he assured me.

"We are in Berlin, right?"

"Of course!"

After more coffee a downstairs neighbor knocked on the door inviting us down for dinner; it was apparently much later than I'd thought.

I rushed out afterwards, shifting my mindset back to where it had been before I met these girls and their bottomless, dark barn beer. I was meant to stay with Luis, who I'd last seen at the Romanian wedding. He was leaving for business in Munich the coming morning, so I'd only get to catch up with him that night.

He gave me a key when he left saying I could stay as long as I wanted. I spent the next day wandering around the city getting a feel for it, discovering currywurst and the like.

Eventually I forged my way back across the big city to the apartment where I'd hazily woken up. One of the girls had gone to pick up my backpack, but she had too many other things to carry and left it behind.

That left me taking the city train for an hour until I arrived in the suburbs to get it myself. I braced myself for the encounter with Lena, who'd be meeting me at the station. I'd been told I was making out with this girl, but who knows what else transpired. One of the other original three girls — who I'd seen that hazy morning and who also failed to retrieve my backpack — seemed to give me a cold vibe. I decided not to read too much into it.

A car rolled up and I could see Lena smiling, she

parked and jumped up, hugging the doubt out of me straight away.

"How are you?" she asked excitedly as she popped the trunk open.

I was as relieved to see my backpack intact as I was to see her cheerful demeanor. I'd been living on the go for four years at that point and had never been separated from my bag like that. Even black-out drunk I was perplexed how I would have left it behind.

"It was so great meeting you and a lot of fun this weekend," she bubbled. "Give me a call in the next few days, I'm sure something will be going on."

She hopped back in and drove off, leaving me to the long ride back to the city center. I was relieved that she was in good spirits, but still wishing I had the clear memories she was smiling about.

Two days later one of Luis' housemates gave me a ride halfway to Munich to a town where he was moving. I never did catch up with Lena or anyone else from that weekend afterwards. Sometimes you gotta keep on down the road to let the next escapade unfold.

BELGIAN QUAD

Of all the Belgian styles, the Trappist subset of their beers are the best known. There was one in particular whose reputation was enough for me to hitch my way into the countryside for some enlightening swigs.

Trappist beers are brewed by monks within the walls of their monasteries. Most, like Chimay, Rochefort, and Orval, make their bottles available in grocery stores and bars around the planet. The only exception — the one that doesn't distribute their beer at all — is Westvleteren.

To taste their beer, one must visit the abbey in person (or be lucky enough to meet someone who smuggled some out). The Belgian Quad they brew — Westvleteren 12 — has been revered by many as the best beer on the planet.

With little time left before leaving the continent, my mission to the abbey became the top priority.

I was in France with ten days left before my flight; I was going from Germany to New York City for a childhood friend's wedding.

My friend Maxy and I had hitched south from Amsterdam to Paris together. We walked barefoot through the highfalutin streets on a lighthearted whim, taking it in before going our separate ways.

I'd met Maxy at the same time I'd met Warren, up in Alaska a few years prior. It was the three of us together who hitched from there to Vancouver, forming a lifelong bond fueled by run-ins around the world like this one.

Maxy was flying from Paris back to home in Australia, leaving me focused on the mission ahead.

I crawled out of my sleeping bag and through the trees I'd hidden in the night we parted, back to the side of the road. My thumb pointed north towards Belgium.

A salesman driving a convertible set the tone for an easy day. Next, a couple of Moroccan guys scooped me up from a petrol station heading straight to Brussels where a friend of mine lived — a simple two-ride day.

Over the past few months I'd passed through Belgium several times, staying with my friend Kasey there in Brussels. Westvleteren notwithstanding, I'd already sampled much of what the country had to offer.

The beer culture in Belgium could be seen as the antithesis to that of the neighboring Germans. Both have a reputation for their meticulousness in brewing that goes back for centuries, but the similarities stop there.

Across the border they're happy to guzzle mellow beer in steins by the liter. The Belgians are more likely to sip from goblets with alcohol levels closer to wine — in the area of 10% abv or higher. They also have no qualms when it comes to using non-traditional ingredients, like candi sugar and even fruit.

Like the previous times at Kasey's, I took full advantage of the many beers available. This three-day break was filled with bottle store runs, late night biking to beer cafes and corner store drop-ins for more beer with snacky samosas.

Keeping it moving and inching my way towards Westvleteren, I next hitched a short ride to the city of Gent. I didn't know anyone there, but found a host using "Couchsurfing." The website lets travelers find locals with a couch or spare room to stay in for a night or more. There's no money exchanged, just good vibes and hospitality.

Before dark I got to Marc's, the student I'd found on Couchsurfing living in a small apartment downtown.

He was a dumpster diver, or a "Freegan." Over that summer I'd met a lot Freegans across Europe. They'd hit up dumpsters outside grocery stores right after closing. Inside they'd dig out any still-good food that legally had to be thrown away, usually due to an upcoming expiration date. Freegans would also go to farmer's markets and bakeries that were shutting down for the day and ask to take whatever would otherwise be trashed.

He was examining some brussel sprouts when I walked in after a day of wandering the city.

"How do these look to you?" he questioned, squinting at one as he rolled it around in his fingers. "I spotted them on the bike ride home."

"They look like brussel sprouts," I shrugged, juggling a few bottles I'd picked up for us.

"Beer?" I offered, holding up a bottle.

I grabbed some glasses and poured while he cooked up the brussel sprouts along with other treasures he'd found. We lived.

Brugge was a city he recommended I check out before my Westvleteren pilgrimage, and only a forty-minute drive further west. I left my gear at his place and hitched two frictionless rides into its massive pedestrian center.

It was more grandiose compared to Gent; I felt as if I was in an open-air museum. People were crossing in all directions, snapping pictures or hurrying along. Statues were plentiful and every building was ornate. I marveled at a huge wall of beers accompanied by a nearby store — a beer museum of sorts.

I hitched a ride back to Gent even easier than when I'd left, with a couple guys and their dog. My traveling lifestyle intrigued them, and in turn they were inspired to tell me everything about their home city, Gent. I was in no hurry, so we drove around as they pointed out the windows, rattling off historic and personal stories.

They parked their car and we continued the impromptu tour on foot through the cobblestone streets past churches, castles and the like. On the edge of the biggest square we ended at a cafe where they prolonged our conversation for the duration of a beer.

On the walk back to Marc's I tried to use an ATM, but the machine laughed at me. It wasn't clear if I was out of money or running into an international usage error. Either way it meant I had to stretch the precious few euros I had left in my pocket.

At Marc's place I met the friends he'd invited over. They were cooking a dumpster dinner and drinking moonshine-like booze between games of chess. They laughed at the cardboard sign I made, "Westvleteren," but that was my next and most important destination.

In the morning I deposited some empty bottles so I'd have extra cash for beer once I reached the abbey. I was down to almost nothing; food would have to appear through travel magic or wait until America. Beer was the priority.

The most beautiful girl in Belgium gave me my first ride of the day. Her eyes pierced like vibrant flowers contrasting tall grass on the mountainside. Alas, she was only going a few kilometers, leaving me in an inspired daze.

A trucker snapped me out of it, rolling us past the remaining cityscape. The next car hesitated before pulling over, later admitting, "I've never picked up a lifter before."

I got another short ride from a woman as I was now getting deep into the countryside. An older man pushed me closer, thrilled to hear I was from New York, like his distant nephew.

I walked from there as no more cars were on this farmland road that leads to the monastery. I'd already done a good deal of walking between all the short rides, as I usually prefer to keep moving rather than standing still with a sign or a thumb. This was the longest walk of the day, surrounded by vast fields dotted with the occasional brick house. Then there it was: Westvleteren.

I triumphantly marched in feeling like Frodo coming from my journey. Except I wasn't dealing with some dinky ring — I was here for the beer. A patio in the back provided a view of the stretching fields from my seat at one of the scattered tables.

A dark goblet from the gods was placed before me — the Westvleteren 12. The foamy head looked thick and rich, as if complementing the deep brown of the brew itself. The complex aroma of dark fruit and Belgian yeast esters was already reaching my nose. I lifted the Holy Grail and breathed it in through both my nose and unharnessed grin, further appreciating the sacred nectar in my grasp. At last, I took a hearty sip.

An explosive symphony of the luxuriously full body and deep, flavorful joy ascended into a deafening crescendo. This built to one all-encompassing resonance scientists around the world would later define as the second Big Bang. I was reborn.

Subtle chocolate notes lingered beyond each savored, silky sip.

A second goblet presented itself — the Westvleteren 8 this time. One sip later and I was experiencing a whole new universe being created whose only state of being was Nirvana.

As I relished my final sips, it sunk in that I now only had two euros and pocket change remaining—not enough for a third beer. I wasn't sure how I'd stretch through the next few days, but I would indeed survive. The malted magic had lifted me to a higher level of consciousness.

I floated away from the sacred grounds in a blissful state of mind as rides hoisted me along in a blur.

A guy in a delivery van handed me a few euros as he dropped me back on the main road. I'd be set for at least another meal or two in my final European days. Travel magic comes when the mind is loose and free.

From there a guy picked me up with his silent girlfriend, getting me up the road further still. Lastly, I got picked up by a carpenter who took me to Marc's apartment for one more night in Gent.

Hitchhiking to Dusseldorf — the German city I'd fly out of — was a twisted ordeal. A language barrier with a plumber left me in a confusing spot in Antwerpen that resulted in over an hour of walking to get back on track. Light rain swept in and out as I got my bearings.

A van driver picked me up, but didn't do a whole lot of talking. Somehow we wound up stopping at his house, which was full of rare and beautiful owls. There was no explanation — it remained unclear if he was shy or spoke zero English. He left me on the roadside with a sandwich and a bottle of Coke as I tried to make sense of my day.

A Dutch guy with an unaccountable Irish accent muddied the situation more. I couldn't help but laugh as we both got further lost together in his attempt to get me heading back in the right direction. He finally dropped me off, leaving me no more certain or uncertain if I'd made any progress.

It was a stoner that ended up steering me on course again. Within a few minutes of getting in his car he'd rolled up a spliff for us to smoke as he got me back to a familiar motorway with a clear direction going forward.

Rides from a suit-wearing banker and then a Dusseldorf local got me within a few blocks of my host's apartment.

I walked on up to meet Kristen — yet another contact made through Couchsurfing. She'd seen on my profile I was into beer and had some local bottles chilled and waiting. The brew gods were smiling upon me this week.

The next day was my last full day before my flight. Kristen's neighbor took me around the city on bicycles until she got off work.

While waiting for her I flipped through a book I was reading and out popped a forgotten twenty euro bill I'd been using as a bookmark. Just like that, I was a wealthy man again.

Immediately, though, I thought about West-vleteren and how nice that third (and fourth and fifth) goblet would have been. All the same I was rapturous in my newfound wealth.

Finished with work, Kristen paraded back home with her friend. After making banana pancakes and pouring a round of shots, we were off to town. That evasive twenty had appeared just in time to enjoy some breweries on this final night.

While going through airport security I scratched my bushy beard. Security glanced between me and my sixteen-year-old passport photo. My harmonica caught attention in the X-ray machine, as it always did. I burned up the last of my magic euros on one last basic altbier before getting on the plane.

I felt a great sense of satisfaction. In Belgium, I'd anointed my system with one of the greatest beers on the planet. I'd also established a baseline of malty expectations across the rest of the continent. European beer culture would continue to evolve as they squinted across the Atlantic for inspiration. I'd be back, many times, to continue imbibing the global beer revolution.

NORTHWESTERN IPA

I'd come to northwest Washington to see a girl on a whim. Despite a transcendent day and night, we simply weren't in sync to go any further.

"Bad timing," as she aptly said.

I watched down the dirt drive as her tail lights dimmed into a blissful haze.

I woke up in a trailer parked in the barn where she'd left me. It belonged to someone she knew who likely wouldn't notice or care about my being there.

Lifting my pack, I started down the same dirt drive towards the road that led to everywhere. I had no schedule, no appointments, no one expecting me and no one who even had a clue where I was.

I reveled in the freedom of these moments, but also knew that most magic occurs when there's a semblance of a plan, rather than total ambivalence. The plan doesn't have to matter or be well-defined,,but there's no diversions without direction.

On the map I'd found a town called Leavenworth, right smack in the middle of the state. I knew nothing else about it and hadn't heard of it before, but liked that it appeared to be surrounded by raw wilderness. It seemed like the type of place where I could camp and get some coffee shop writing done by day — perhaps spend a week or so in this fashion.

Leavenworth would further prove that plans are rarely as interesting as opportunity.

A passing cyclist stopped to inform me that the free Whidbey Island bus I was waiting for didn't run on Sundays. No matter, the thumb cares not of the names of days, and neither did the Thai woman driving my way.

After her, I was lifted by a Navy sailor taking his visiting mother to Deception Pass. I'd admired this high bridge when first rolling onto the island, on the free bus. I breathed in the distance to the rocky cliffs rising to the forested clusters.

I sauntered above the water as if passing through a portal to the next phase. A trail off the road lead me through the woods wrapping around a quiet lake. Camping there crossed my mind, but my momentum made the thought of sticking around unbearable, even in the face of the serene surroundings.

Instead I caught a ride from a homebuilder who

was contemplating making some changes in his life, which he admitted was becoming boring.

"I have to start living outside the box," he lamented. "Hell, I've spent my life just building big boxes."

He brought me to Everett where I found a path to cut through the city on foot. While sitting by the river a cyclist and his dog joined me. He'd rigged a motor on his bicycle and had plans of selling kits with solar panels. He appreciated my version of travel, saying he'd one day do the same with his modified solar-bike method.

I kept walking, getting to the inland road towards Leavenworth. Two guys driving across town scooped me up, hopping me up on energy drinks that kept me buzzing along.

Beginning with the gentle bliss of a spring love hangover, my day had eased into a forested meander towards a soft destination.

I walked, sang, and spun on down the hill, thumb out and back-trotting whenever a car came passing. Soon I was bounding down to hop in a woman's car who'd stopped for me, driving me on to the next town.

An outdoorsman named George stopped for me there.

"I've done my share of walking," he told me. "I know what it's like."

"Yeah," I agreed. "But it's beautiful around here and I'm in no big hurry, just going to see what Leavenworth is all about."

Being Mother's Day, he was heading to her house for dinner — a dozen more miles towards Leavenworth. He dropped some things off at his house, grabbed some beer from the store and we were off.

"You can come for dinner if you want, my mom loves visitors," he said, passing me a beer. "Then you could sleep on the couch at my house after. It's messy, but it's something."

I like questions with simple answers.

We shot up the mountain, passing a great waterfall and arriving at the tucked away house. His mother was talkative and indeed excited for the unexpected guest.

I met George's girlfriend, too. The four of us walked along the river that ran past the house before having a delicious pork feast.

Back at George's, he stocked me up on snacks, gave me some fire kindling, a giant knife and other tidbits he thought would be useful. In the morning he drove me to the road, back on my way again.

As if things weren't already going well, next Vince picked me up. He was a long-haired musician and contractor coming from the coast, on his way to Leavenworth.

"For some good old-fashioned work," he told me.

He was clearing property for a woman before building her house.

We cruised over the mountain pass — another great drive — talking about his twelve-piece band among other things.

As we pulled closer to town, he offered me a

day's work clearing wood piles.

"I was supposed to have another friend to help us, but he didn't pick up his phone this morning," he sighed. "I can only pay you a hundred bucks, but it's something. No guarantees, but if she says it's OK then I'd love the help."

We exchanged numbers and he dropped me off in town, saying he'd call me later after confirming with the owner.

With a nose for good beer, it didn't take long to stumble upon Icicle Brewery a few blocks away. They specialized in German-beers, although had many other styles to choose from too. The German lean soon made sense.

The whole town was Bavarian-themed, to a ridiculous degree. To attract visitors they'd made ordinances to transform the town. Even the chains, like McDonalds and Starbucks, had Bavarian-themed signs out front.

It felt like walking through Disney World. It seems corny because it is, but I came to find this town was more about the beautiful outdoors, rafting and community.

I ordered a beer and talked with the bartender and her friend. They pointed out potential camping spots nearby while telling me about the area at large.

I inquired about what I'd seen written on the chalkboard: "Keg scavenger hunt."

"Today's the first day, actually," the bartender said, "It looks really fun!"

"So," she explained. "Each day this week there's a different bar in town you'll have to go to and order a craft beer, then they'll give you a clue."

She pointed to where the first bar was listed.

"By Friday, whoever finds it gets a full keg or a fat bar tab," she said.

Sounded pretty damn awesome to me.

After a couple beers I tracked down a coffee shop and got some writing done, then scarfed down a leftover pork sandwich from last night's dinner.

Across the street and up a staircase I found The Loft — the bar giving out the first keg clue. The bartender handed me a fortune-cookie sized piece of paper and poured me a beer. The clue read:

"NasikElt is where it Got started, literally A namesake that's Dear to both you and me."

We contemplated the clue with the only other guy in the bar, Ryan. The conversation shifted to homebrewing and local beer as more people filed in.

I noticed the girl from the brewery and some familiar faces from the coffee shop. The place filled up, and I was in the center of it. I was getting passed shots and talking to a guy about the bratwurst beer garden he'd opened across the street. At one point I got pulled in for a shotski — a snow ski with five shot glasses glued to it that required a coordinated tilt.

My phone rang in the midst of this — it was Vince with the good news.

"She said it's OK, so do you wanna come help?" he

asked.

"Definitely!", I answered.

"Great, meet me at my motel in the morning and we'll drive out to the site from there."

I finished up my beer, grabbed my pack and headed into the night to camp. I found a spot off the main road in the area the girls had told me about and rolled out my bivy tent.

By early morning I was waking up to a view of the remaining snow on the mountain tops. Vince suggested breakfast when I knocked on his motel room door. Two others who'd be helping, Dennis and his son James, were waiting for us at the cafe.

Vince picked up the tab and we barreled down Icicle road towards the property, Dennis driving the big truck behind us.

The rudimentary driveway crossed over the river before carving up the mountain. Another truck hauling the rented wood chipper was waiting for us there.

That chipper truck got stuck going around a tight turn, but Dennis wrestled it out with the excavator.

The property was in a beautiful spot nestled there in the mountains. The lighthearted woman who owned it was living in a temporary structure closer to the river with her dog.

I spent the day in constant motion, throwing the bigger logs in the chipper and clearing out the piles of trees and debris. The alpine piece of paradise around us kept me smiling the whole way through.

Vince passed me a hundred bucks as we drove away from the site.

"You wanna do it again tomorrow, same deal?" he asked. "I'm in a different motel tonight, I'll call for a room with two beds."

The shower alone was worth it. Dennis and James had the room next door, and after I showered the pounds of dirt off me I joined them on the balcony for a cold beer.

When talk of dinner arose, it was Vince who suggested The Loft. He'd apparently stepped in for a drink the night before, right after he'd called me and I left to make camp.

"I'm buying!" Dennis announced, leaving nothing to chance.

The bartender and the server recognized me as we came in.

"You sure make friends quick," Vince chuckled.

I began exchanging more nods and hello's as the place filled up again. Ryan also popped in and I remembered the scavenger hunt.

After eating, the three of them retreated to the motel. I hung back to finish my beer and get some intel. The clues were being given out at a bar across town, too far for me to reach now.

"Did you get the next clue yet?" I asked Ryan.

He seemed reluctant, but his cagey competitiveness was too awkward to sustain. He passed the clue over to me:

"Hey there JosephIne! How do you do? Do you Remember me my Baby? Like I remember you?"

We dissected it as I finished my beer. I was about to leave when the bartender passed me a whiskey and Coke.

"Made the wrong drink for someone, you want it?" he smiled.

I stayed for the drink and would have stayed even longer, but it felt just as good to crash into the motel bed.

We woke up early, ate a continental breakfast and drove back to the site. The work started the same as the day before, but we had handled most of the smaller debris.

Dennis was using the excavator to move everything around, leaving James and I pacing around.

"Take a load off," Vince told me. "He's got it covered now."

I wandered around the property, leaping up and down the river rocks seeing how far I could go.

Vince gave me another hundred bucks, despite the half-day. We stopped to smoke a joint along the river, then Dennis and James split back to the coast.

Vince was also heading that way, but offered to get me a beer at the brewery beforehand.

We sat at a high-top on the patio. The server swooped over when she noticed me, giggling about the shotski from the other night.

"You really do know the whole town!" Vince said.

He stayed for just a few minutes before we said

our goodbyes and mutual thanks, leaving me with a full beer.

With my backpack by my feet, I held my glass in quiet contemplation. I was on my own again, free for whatever. Perhaps I'd get to all the writing I'd been thinking about.

Two grinning girls then came over to my table.

"Hey! Are you traveling?" the blonde one asked me.

They'd come from a group of half a dozen people a couple tables over.

"Yeah," I smiled, "I just hitchhiked over the pass from the coast a couple days ago."

"You're a hitchhiker!?" asked the brunette as she lit up. "So are we!"

They told me how they'd hitched around the country together during the summer. I thought about how easy it must have been (and it was). They were both vibrant, pretty and full of energy while still appearing laid-back.

Amy was the blonde one who'd grown up in Leavenworth. She had a warm smile and the understanding eyes of an old friend.

"What are you doing here in town?" she asked.

It was a good question, one that was being answered moment by moment. I told them what I'd done so far with Vince and the keg scavenger hunt I'd taken on. Coincidentally, they were heading to the Mexican restaurant down the street next, which is where that night's clue was being given out.

I joined the rest of their group in the corner. They

were all living in Vail, but were staying with Amy's parents for a week to see the area.

We headed down the block together for drinks, tacos and the all-important clue — one step closer to finding my treasure.

"The tributariEs. The tributaries. Oh, how they are vast. The Hunt starts at the beginning or would it be the lasT?"

During dinner they offered to let me stay with them; Riley even picked up my tab. She was wearing pink rimmed sunglasses that couldn't hide her curiosity — she was wanderer through and through.

We brought a case of beer to the house, then sat around a fire in the backyard by the river. Stories flew back and forth as I made some new friends.

In the morning they suggested that I stay another couple of days. I laid in the sun with Amy and Riley a while swapping hitchhiking stories. I also started thinking about my next move after Leavenworth.

Ever since I got north of California, on my way to the girl in Washington, people were telling me about Bend, Oregon. The town seemed to get brought up whenever I expressed an interest in craft beer.

A search for hosts in Bend on the Couchsurfing website turned up a surprising name — Billy Jackson.

I knew Billy as a brewer in Salt Lake City, a mutual friend with Camille and Carl. His number was saved in my phone, so I rang him straight away.

"Kenny!" he answered.

Sure enough, he was living in Bend working at a new brewery that head-hunted him out of Salt Lake.

"My home is your home, come stay as long as you want," he told me.

Coincidentally, my birthday was three days later, which I shared with him exactly to the year. I now knew where I was heading next.

With that sorted, I skipped by the brewery to see which bar was giving out the next clue. They directed me to a spot just around the corner.

I got there only ten minutes after they opened, ordered my beer and got my clue:

> "To the north a <u>R</u>ainbow is seen in the cold
> And to the south the gates ar<u>E</u> pearly and bol<u>D</u>"

"Has anyone else been in?" I asked the bartender.

I was just making conversation, I knew they'd just opened minutes ago. I also wasn't sure if anyone, besides Ryan and I, knew about or gave a damn about finding the hidden keg in this little town.

"There's been a few just before you," she surprised me.

I now had a sense of urgency, but this latest clue was making things fall into place. I gathered it was under a bridge, that much was certain. The underlined letters backwards so far spelled "DER THE BRIDGE."

I downed my beer and darted into the park nearby. I crawled under every bridge I could find.

The latest clue clicked once I learned that Rainbow Falls froze in the winter for ice climbing.

I ran out to Icicle Road and hitched a ride heading the same direction as the property we'd been clearing. Halfway there was the hiking trail with a big bridge at the start.

I searched below on both sides of the river, twice. Then three times. The clues seemed undeniable, but I saw nothing.

I hiked for shy of an hour all the way to the climbing face — no bridges up there. I came back down, scouring the main bridge again; still nothing. Across the street I climbed to where the ice falls would solidify in winter — no bridges on that side.

I was perplexed, although impressed with the beautiful scenery and hiking I'd just subjected myself to. The clues made it seem so certain it was under the main bridge I'd checked.

Confused, I hit the road, hitching a ride back to the brewery with a couple who'd been hiking as well. I tried to coax some extra clues out of the bartender, but she knew less than I did.

Retreating to Amy's, I'd have to be patient until the final clue was revealed the next day.

In the late morning, I had her, Riley and the others on board. Our mission was to find this damn keg, now with the benefit of their car.

The next bar didn't open until late afternoon. We spent a couple hours beforehand driving around, checking underneath every bridge in town. We rechecked the main bridge the clues pointed to, in case they weren't hiding it until this final day. Nope. Still not there.

We reached the bar minutes after it opened. As we approached, a guy came screaming out past us — he was after it!

We matched his frantic pace as we scrambled in to order a beer, chugging it together as they handed us the final clue.

"You think you know but one more piece you Need
The last of a map to reveal the treasures key
Get your clues in order have them to read
Make sure to register bUt forget paying the fee."

This last clue only further confirmed that it was under the bridge I'd thought, but now there was a note about the registration box.

As we raced outside, a group of guys drinking in the corner asked us what the commotion was about.

"There's this keg scavenger hunt thing, this was the final clue," I told them. "We gotta run for it!"

We gunned it back to the bridge. They hurried under while I ripped into the registration box. Empty.

The guy who'd screamed past us was already underneath scratching his head as well. We turned looking dumbly at each other, stumped and stunned.

At this point I called the brewery.

"Has someone found the keg?" I asked.

And someone had. I couldn't believe it. We drove straight over.

"Where was it?" I asked.

It was under that damn bridge. The bartender pointed us to the brewer who'd actually hidden it. I told him how I'd checked there yesterday and just now, and found nothing.

He ended up pouring us a round of consolation beers. It was their first time trying this scavenger hunt and he was stoked that we were into it. I was still perplexed.

Later, we were at a beer garden a couple blocks away when I overheard a group of guys on the sidewalk talking about the keg.

"Hey!" I shouted, getting their attention from up behind the railing. "Do you know who found the keg?"

"We did!" they shouted.

"What?! When did you find it?" I asked, "I was looking under that bridge all day yesterday and today."

Suddenly, they looked familiar.

"We got the clue before they opened on Thursday," they admitted. "We ran over there and pulled it out of the river, it was on the near side attached with a chain."

These sons of bitches. Now I knew why they looked familiar. This was the same group at the final bar who'd asked us what we were doing — mocking us and everyone else dashing in, knowing they had it in the bag already.

We cursed their names, but the night carried on beautifully, despite their cheat. After all, we'd at least gotten a free round from the brewery. Also, the beer garden we were at now was owned by the guy I'd met at The Loft nights earlier. He kicked me a free liter of beer and bratwurst before we continued bar hopping.

Riley gave me a ride to the far edge of town the following day to get me started towards Bend.

After hopping out of one car I was running up a hill to catch a truck who'd stopped at the top for me. I stepped in, out of breath, but elated to hear that he'd be passing through Bend three hours down the road.

I found Billy downtown, he'd been mobbing from bar to bar with a big group of friends and co-workers.

"So, I got you some work if you want it," he told me after a few beers. "We've got a new bottling line and it's pretty finicky, so they could probably use your help for a few days. All cash."

Paid to be in a brewery — sometimes life is easy. I'd spend the next couple of weeks assembling six-packs, going to beer events, and parlaying conversations about string theory into make-out sessions.

Sometimes you miss out on the keg, but good times flow for those that keep moving.

RYEWAY 117

October is the peak of the outdoor marijuana harvest in California. I stumbled upon the scene early in my travels and could make my money for the year in as little as a few weeks.

Over the years and seasons I helped all over the state, but Chico became a homebase at times.

My friend Warren first convinced me to hitchhike there with him from the Bay Area to see a friend of his. That friend — Dana — and Sierra Nevada Brewery are what defined the town.

Dana had been in Chico when the owner of the now legendary brewery was still fiddling around with homebrews and dairy equipment in the 1970s. She drank wine and cared little for beer, but she loved Sierra Nevada because she loved Chico. She also had a knack for connecting people with whoever or whatever she thought may enrich them.

"You *need* to go to Beer Camp," she'd scold me with bewilderment as if I was a child refusing to go to his best friend's birthday party.

Her red wine splashed securely within in her clutched tumbler glass as she glared at me with loving shock from across her coffee table.

"Kenny!" she jolted, unreceptive to excuses.

"I know, I know," I'd admit, lifting my pint glass in reflection.

I got this speech from Dana every harvest season, and every other odd time I dropped into town.

Beer Camp was heralded as an all-expenses-paid hands-on trip to the brewery — a Willy Wonka type of experience. Those lucky enough to win the contest got to brew their own dreamt-up batch of beer using Sierra's equipment.

Dana was right of course — there was no justifiable reason for me not to enter. I thought it was too good to be true, too much of a longshot to win.

The year came that she convinced me. In turn, I talked my beer-loving friend in Sacramento, Aaron, into entering with me.

I imagined how amazing it would be if we won, but I couldn't have predicted the adventure it would spark in the aftermath.

We needed to submit videos — short and entertaining pleas — that would get voted on by employees and the public.

The best film ever produced is "Dumb & Dumber." Hard-facts like this are excellent footholds amidst a world of uncertainty. We reenacted scenes from the movie adapted to our mission to get to Beer Camp, then hoped for the best.

"So you're telling me there's a chance?"

By standing on the shoulders of dumber giants — and after weeks of waiting — we won! Camp was a month away, starting the first week of December.

With harvest wrapped up and Beer Camp looming, I spent the time hitching around California, wild with anticipation. I dropped in on nearby friends, made some new ones and bounced around as usual.

With three days until camp I'd traveled as far down as San Diego and up to my sister's apartment in Hollywood. If I made it to Aaron's in Sacramento we'd ride up to camp in Chico together.

A middle-aged, missile-defense employee heading three hundred miles to Manteca seemed like a great start. And after several hours of conversation, he offered to let me crash at his place for the night and run me up the last hour to Aaron's in the morning.

He cooked up a big dinner when we got to his two-story home in the suburbs. What he lacked in beer, he tried to make up for with wine.

It wasn't until later — as he sat across from me naked in the hot tub — that I realized he may have had an ulterior motive. The intentional awkward pauses were a strong hint. The wine, hot tub suggestion and nudity stood as solid supporting evidence.

I harnessed my prior obliviousness until he gave up on pouring.

He delivered on the ride to Sacramento in the morning, but his enthusiasm level had knocked down a peg.

The sight of Aaron and his wife Jess homebrewing in their garage was a beautiful thing. Glasses of past homebrews in hand, I hopped out of the car and onto the next scene.

"We're really doing it though, aren't we buddy?"

We shot up the road in Aaron's car with our golden tickets glowing like pints of pale ale in the sun. Our adrenaline fizzed like carbonation, foaming up as we poured into Chico with the realization that this was actually happening.

The town fizzed with a static-electric decadence as we rolled in, like running through empty high school classrooms in your teenage summertime.

The high-ceilinged taproom of Sierra Nevada welcomed us with outgoing "camp counselors" pointing us to an open bar. We gulped down beers as other campers trickled in. Most were recognizable from the videos they'd submitted.

There was Jim from right there in Chico. Besides Aaron, there were two others also from Sacramento. Jameson, a special effects editor, came up from LA. A chemist and a skydiver each came from the Bay Area. John from Chicago seemed to like the Blackhawks more than beer. Andy came down from Salem and Stephanie from Portland. Scot, a more serious homebrewer than many of us, had come from north of Seattle, in Bellingham.

For three days we were showered with beer from every tap, cellar and hidden barrel throughout the brewery. They took us to rooms with bales of hops piled to the ceilings. We cycled their beer bike through the gardens that supplied their restaurant. In their laboratories we performed quality control on some of the never-ending flow of beer they produced.

Between all this we feasted in their taproom and were treated to excursions to bars in town. We went to a nearby monastery that made wine. We danced to live music in their venue and met the other lucky Beer Camp group who arrived a day after us.

Many of us were homebrewers and had thought ahead. Back at the hotel each night we'd crack open our own bottles to share, as if we hadn't gotten enough beer already.

The apex of the experience was to brew a beer of our own creation using their equipment and guidance. After much deliberation, we dialed in our masterpiece: a 7.5% hoppy honey rye ale we dubbed "Ryeway 117." The "117" referenced our somewhat arbitrary group number.

Equally hungover as we were buzzed, we giddily shoveled hops onto carts and weighed out grains. Buckets of local honey arrived right on cue as the brew session began. All the while we were dreaming of the magical beer it would ferment into — and the celebrations to follow.

By the end, my fellow campers were scattering to cars and airports in a mass exodus. Only Stephanie and I clung to an extra day, piggybacking a few more beer sessions with the group behind us.

When it was all over I was left to nurse a couple day's worth of a hangover on a friend's couch in town. I mentally geared up for a cold December hitch east towards New York. After the holidays, I'd spend awhile hitching around the country, patiently waiting.

Sierra's finale was to ship two kegs of Ryeway to each camper's local bar for a release party, plus one personal keg to do with what they wanted.

"Cheers Jim!" I smiled when the moment came.

We milked one more beat to breathe in the spicy hop aroma of the sacred golden nectar before taking the first victorious swig.

Bound to no address — and very eager — I picked up my keg right from the brewery. Jim was the lone camper living in Chico, so together we were the first to raise glasses of the glowing masterpiece.

The spicy, sweet, hop-kicked bliss-bomb lit me up, plastering a smile to my face that would remain for weeks and miles of the adventure to come.

Days later, Ryeway appeared on tap at the brewery itself. I was waiting at the doors when they opened like a kid on Christmas morning.

I proudly admired "Ryeway 117" written on their chalkboard and paper menus. They'd even designed a glowing, buzzing black bee against a golden honeycomb.

Stationed on a bar stool in front of the custom

tap handle, I put in my version of an eight-hour work day. I drank glass after glass of our potion as friends took shifts joining me. Jim dropped in and counselors came to clink glasses.

I was euphoric; all was right with the world.

With great mobility comes great responsibility. I wanted to clink glasses with all my fellow campers — or as many as possible. Being that most were on the West Coast, I set my mind to it.

I wouldn't be alone on this endeavor. A beer-loving girl with electric-blue eyes — Marilyn — was along for the ride.

We'd hitched together around the U.S. and Mexico the previous summer, back when her hair was short and bleached blonde. By winter she recoiled back to work in Indiana where we'd first hit it off a year before that.

The long, cold and grinding months were in stark contrast to the sunny, freewheeling hitching days of summer together. So much so that she quit her job all together.

Back at my side again, now with her natural auburn-colored hair, she was equally excited for the beer-filled mission ahead.

We'd have to get down to Jameson in Los Angeles, north of Seattle to Scot, and to everyone between as the Ryeway reached them.

Back-to-back nights of release parties fired off in Sacramento, the second being Aaron's at his go-to beer bar in Folsom. Along with the kegs, Sierra Nevada sent a representative to pass out free shirts, hats and add to the party.

Together Aaron and I poured the first pints before a cheering bar full of thirsty believers. We beamed with pride as ourselves and others indulged in the mighty Ryeway 117 — sip, swig, gulp, and guzzle as the night roared on.

It felt as if we'd been selected as Nobel laureates in chemistry. We'd created a euphoric liquid suitable for the Holy Grail — designed for the gods, yet accessible to the common man fortunate enough to cross its flow.

Hunter, a fellow camper and an actual chemist, hosted the first of the next back-to-back parties in the Bay Area. After a few hair-of-the-dog recovery days in Sacramento, we made it over there to Berkeley.

In the sanctity of Hunter's local bar, surrounded by his closest friends (and lucky walk-ins), Marilyn and I once again dosed ourselves with Ryeway by the pintful.

The next day we hitched a short ride to Walnut Creek for Marcel's party. Towards the evening he and his friends swooped into his spacious bar like the skydivers they were. We bopped around the giant venue full of rye and luster.

Every sip was taken with voracious gratitude, flinging me to the far reaches of the perceived universe and back to the bar again as I gulped it down.

As the party dwindled, we downed our final pints like fuel, then ripped out to the darkened cityscape.

Unlike the prior night, where we slept in Hunter's living room, this night we were winging it. Neither of us had thought to seek a Couchsurfing host or make a strong effort to provoke an invitation from someone at the bar.

For over an hour we prowled down the sidewalks of the urban sprawl. Our trained eyes scanned for any hideaway, any patch of trees or any hidden nook suitable to stealth-camp. There was nothing.

As cars drove by we stuck out our thumbs in an impossible attempt to inch our way towards Sacramento. Aaron had convinced us to come volunteer at a beer festival there before moving on.

Feeling exhausted, Marilyn unsheathed her phone to seek a cheap hotel and hail an Uber using banked free-credits.

A driver rolled up shortly. The sixty-something-year-old with a relaxed face chatted away as we climbed in, curious why we were in such a strange part of town at this late hour.

"We were at a party and gonna try to hitchhike back to Sacramento," I started, "but it's kinda hard to catch rides this late, and didn't seem like we could find anywhere to camp around here either."

"You live in Sacramento?" he asked.

"No, no — my friend does," I replied. "I'm from New York originally and she's from Indiana. We're living out of our backpacks at the moment, traveling all over the place, just running around having fun."

"That's fantastic!" he said, perking up even more than he already was. "Well, this was going to be my last ride of the night, I'm heading back home to Sacramento. I can just 'turn off the meter' and take you with if you'd like."

I looked back at Marilyn who was beaming as much as I was.

"Sure!" I answered for us.

After more than an hour of back-and-forth stories, he was dropping us off at Aaron's, only several blocks from where he himself lived.

I'm endlessly amazed by the road's propensity for serendipity.

We went with Aaron and his wife to the beer festival a day later. We joined volunteers setting up and pouring beers at one of the many booths. In exchange, we got to run around sampling the West Coast breweries' goods ourselves. Nothing as epic as the Ryeway of course, but the next release party was just over a week away in Santa Monica.

With the time to spare we decided we'd first take a detour to the north of San Francisco, enticed by several great breweries.

The breakaway ride from Sacramento was a guy our age heading home to Santa Rosa. He kept us entertained with stories of his ancestors engaging in duels and how his mother trained the whale "Bubbles" from SeaWorld.

He unloaded us in front of Russian River Brewery. Over the next few days, we hitched a slew of lightning rides up and down the highway and backroads to the breweries on our list. Each night we set up the tent in whatever hidden patch of forest we could find.

Around Petaluma, we got back into go-mode for the four-hundred mile plunge south. My sister in Hollywood was the next target.

Late in the day, we'd hitched as far as the northern entrance to the Golden Gate bridge. A tourist bus outfitted to look like a trolley car slowed down with one of the guides hanging off the side when he noticed my outstretched thumb.

"Hurry, get on!" he shouted. "We're not supposed to do this. Come on!"

We climbed in amongst the tourists, laughing with each other as we breezed over the bridge into San Francisco. Once on the other side the driver stopped the bus and jogged back to us smiling.

"Where are you two going?" he asked.

"Los Angeles!" I exclaimed. "Thanks for the lift!"

"OK, OK," he smiled back. "I know the right place to leave you."

He ran back to the wheel to keep the tour going smooth. We crept through the Presidio as he remarked over the loudspeakers about the military housing. Tourists took their obligatory photos while otherwise ignoring the two hitchhikers who'd crashed the party.

When he signaled for us to hop off, we were on the 101. This "highway" technically goes clear down to Los Angeles, but here in the heart of the city it was like being on any other street. It wasn't an effective place to hitchhike from, but at least we were over the bridge

The last breath of the sun was steady exhaling, and while we considered trying to push on, grabbing a pint of beer seemed much more prudent. It was also, incidentally, my birthday. For this reason, Marilyn found us a cheap room so we could enjoy the night and delay the grind out of the city.

Hitchhiking out of the Bay Area, or any major city sprawl, is like trudging through a swamp. Tight spots make it difficult for cars to pull over and they often aren't going far (not realizing even a "short" ride can save hours of walking).

Fearful suspicion runs high when drivers clump hitchhikers in with the homeless, hustlers and undefinable strangers.

Police are more present and have the potential to slow you down — regardless of the law. This makes walking on the highway a last ditch effort that's bound to be a short-lived attempt.

We soaked in the night, slept well and faced the day. After several hours of this urban bush-whacking we'd only covered twenty-five miles. There in Hayward, an unfamiliar brewery caught our eye — we jumped at the chance to take a break.

The shuffleboard table was more memorable than the beer itself. Next to the highway, we dropped into a diner to delay our city-escape a bit longer.

As we cozied into a booth we were approached by the curious manager. The sight of our backpacks had triggered his nostalgia. He clung to us while recalling a swirl of stories from his days motorcycling around the country years ago.

We left full of food without being allowed to pay. The good vibes of his generosity carried over into a quick ride to Tracy where we were decidedly out of the worst of the urban muck.

A truck driver going a significant distance — finally — lifted us up from there.

"We used to do crash 'em up derbys," he told us as we cruised through the desert. "We'd gather up some vehicles and go into an empty lot and have at it."

In his earlier days, he loved stealing cars and had been busted for armed robbery, among other things.

"Just smashing into each other?" I asked.

"You bet!" he reminisced with resurrected joy. "Those cars were unrecognizable after."

He was grinning backward in time, then shaking his head with a tempered acknowledgement of his changed ways. He'd spent seventeen years boxed up in a jail not all that far from where we were driving.

When he forked east to Bakersfield we were left making a token attempt to hitch another ride under the darkened sky. With fewer headlights coming and no cover for camping, Marilyn once again pointed us towards the light of a motel.

The expense of hotels, motels and even hostels are ones I try to avoid in my travels. Marilyn, however, was less concerned with money. She didn't mind camping in some pretty strange spots — in fact she loved it — but didn't have as much patience for the search.

I learned not to argue. Nights like San Francisco and now this night were undeniably simpler and more enjoyable.

Feeling well-rested, we hitched a direct ride to Hollywood in the morning.

My younger sister shares the same birthday as me — eight years apart — and we arrived in time for belated celebration with her friends. Altogether Marilyn and I would spend a few days around LA, crashing on the floor of my sister's studio apartment.

Jameson's release party was a couple nights away in neighboring Santa Monica, but we were keen to spin down through San Diego first. We geared up to face the hitchhiking muckery of the Los Angeles sprawl, which is even worse than the Bay Area. Every ride feels like an unlikely miracle, and often only going several miles before the next junction in the highway spaghetti.

We indeed hitched the shortest ride possible from a woman who took us just one exit to Sunset Boulevard. All she wanted was to warn us of the dangers of hitchhiking and the certain murderers waiting to pick us up.

In a matter of minutes, our murderer picked us up. He forced us to eat at a Chinese restaurant on his dime before driving us to Oceanside. The two-hour ride took us clear past all of Los Angeles and Orange County.

Our next killer ride came from a "back in my day" type of guy in his classic car. He excluded Marilyn and me from our own "doomed generation," citing that our hitchhiking spirit excepted us from such.

Our killer had spare time after a failed fishing trip, so chattily detoured us to White Labs — a prominent yeast manufacturer.

To show off their yeast they opened a small taproom. They brew small batches that are separated with different yeast strains to each ferment independently. Beer nerds can come and taste the unique difference each yeast imparts on what's otherwise the exact same batch of beer.

The previous summer we'd stopped in for a few of these tasting trays before leaving on foot to the highway. Back at that time we were hitchhiking east towards Nogales and into Mexico. After thirty minutes of waiting a car stopped — it was the White Labs bartender. She lived in Ocean Beach, but embraced the harmony of happenstance by boosting us eastbound a couple dozen miles.

We were happy to walk in this time — nearly a year later — to see she was working again. She recognized us as well. Not too many backpacked couples were popping through the isolated entrance of this nerdy beer haven.

We knocked out a couple sampler trays again just before she got off her shift. We were also heading for Ocean Beach this time around, so she happily gave us a lift all the way. No walking or hitchhiking needed. We revelled in the magic of timing and connection that propagates throughout any good ramble.

We slid out in front of Pizza Port. The Southern California brewery chain happened to be the weekly meetup location for locals on the Couchsurfing website.

After a couple of beers we had a girl offering us a bed to sleep in following the night of bar hopping.

We stuck with her the next day, biking around cliffs and tidal pools before the inevitable visit to Stone Brewery.

We hitched a sunset ride up to my brother's in Oceanside for the night, then were right back to the road the morning of Jameson's release party.

Again we received a generous lift from someone compelled by curiosity who had time on their hands. He drove us clear through the sprawling Orange County and Los Angeles nonsense straight to Santa Monica. It seemed the power of the Ryeway had made us immune to the typical stuck-sparge of Southern California hitchhiking.

By nightfall, we were with Jameson and his friends at his favorite bar. Again, there was a representative from Sierra Nevada passing out hats, shirts and other trinkets. Most importantly though, Ryeway 117 was flowing strong. I'd missed my hopped honey splendor. The world was whole again.

I positioned my party two nights later at another bar in Santa Monica; Sierra shipped the kegs to make it happen.

My sister joined with her friends and the Ryeway gravitated Jameson in for another session as well. Shuffleboard pucks slid down the table while the spicy rye notes tantalized taste buds for another flourishing bout with the spellbinding brew.

Our thumbs were flashing out again the very next morning as the next party was up in Salem, Oregon.

Despite our eagerness, we waited for hours until a car pulled over — followed by a Hollywood cop.

"You better hurry!" the cop yelled, mercifully motioning for us to go ahead and take the ride.

But the spooked car retreated into traffic without us.

"I didn't mean to scare him off," the cop shouted over, now looking shy.

He hesitated, then drove off himself without another word. I figured he'd come to check us out, because of boredom or sense of responsibility. Our excitement, followed by deflation, had somehow legitimized us.

Our patience paid off, and we started chaining short rides together. We piled into a minivan next to a bunch of kids heading to Santa Clarita — the northern edge of the Southern California sinkhole.

With all the long waits the sky had already gone dark, so we made camp in the forested hills.

There's nothing but wide-open northbound from there, so it was no surprise that our first early morning ride was heading to the Bay Area.

The second ride was just as long, but less expected. Liam was the driver, heading up to Arcata on the northern coast. He was as happy as us, letting Marilyn take the wheel for a stint so he could relax.

By the time we reached Arcata he'd offered to let us set up our tent in his backyard. We arrived to meet his brother, who was skeptical of us at first. It turned out he used to work for a brewery though, and our talk of beer translated to trust.

Liam surrendered us to his brother's old brewery in the morning, Mad River — we thanked him for the ride and hospitality. We took a personal tour to discover they were using some of Sierra Nevada's original equipment. This seemed like a good omen.

From there we hitched chunk rides further up the last of California feeling breezy. One guy who picked us up even wanted to stop into a brewery called Six Rivers before driving us further north.

As it got dark, we crammed into one more car overflowing with people and camping gear en route to a regional rainbow gathering.

One of the dreadlocked guys told us how he once lived up in the branches of a tree for six months to protect it from getting cut down. A support group would bring him food, supplies and handle his toilet-bucket. Authorities occasionally climbed up, he told us, trying to remove him. For this situation there was a box secured to the tree he could lock his hands inside so they couldn't pull him off.

When he finally came down he spent some time in jail and the tree got cut down. He treated this last bit like an unimportant footnote. If not for my curious questioning I imagine he would have left that out altogether.

By mid-morning we leisurely emerged from our woodland dormitory to catch our first ride of the day — over the border into Oregon. On the raw coastline of Northern California — and up through Oregon to Washington — finding hidden camping spots is as effortless as the hitchhiking.

We breezed north at the day's gentle pace. For one stretch, we bounced along on the couch of a retired couple's RV. A moment later a vacationing doctor is detouring us around town to see chainsaw art. Next, a man who used to live on the streets of LA is telling us about his settlement money that he'll use to escape to Alaska.

All is welcome when you're not in a hurry; even the waits between rides feel peaceful.

Ultimately we landed at Rogue Brewery in Newport where a couple of Marilyn's friends rendezvoused with us. We spent the next few days at their home in Corvallis, running around all the breweries from there to Eugene.

Despite all the great beer, I remained thirsty for the masterwork.

We got our next hit in Salem, at Andy's party. Stephanie drove down from Portland to join in too. Her party had been weeks earlier, but what was most important was to be together again, raising golden glasses above our thirsty faces. My body needed that injection of hoppy, rye happiness to keep going.

I was getting used to these nights of liquid bliss and now just one remained. Before heading up to see Scot in Bellingham, however, it would've been criminal to pass up Portland.

After a day of kayaking on the river — and another brewery visit — we headed up to the city with one of Marilyn's friends living there.

I was relieved when they made plans to hike around a waterfall I'd been to. For over three solid months Marilyn and I had been in-step throughout the day and sleeping on top of each other at night. All this persistent time together — she'd even slip into the shower with me — was taking a toll.

So while they drove off to the waterfall, I leapt into the city to dance with the love I would never tire of — beer.

Stephanie's friend, John, met me downtown. He'd been to a previous year's Beer Camp and was prolific on the Portland beer scene. Years later he'd cement his legacy by visiting — and drinking at — seventy-seven Portland breweries in a single day. On another occasion, I'd join him in drinking at a mere sixty-one breweries in one day.

On this particular day we weren't setting any records, but good beer was still the motivation. By dark we'd cascaded through a series of the best bars and breweries in town. Stephanie and a gang of others eventually flowed into our malty rampage as well.

Portland was an easy city for Marilyn and I — or

anyone — to get caught up in. The funky vibe, the breweries and the food — like burgers with grilled cheese sandwiches in place of buns — held our attention for a solid week.

On an unavoidable rainy day we hitched north towards Bellingham to complete our mission.

We stayed with two different Couchsurfing hosts with a knack for homebrewing along the way. First for a night in Tacoma, then a couple nights in Seattle.

The last stretch to Bellingham, just ninety miles north of Seattle, took a half dozen rides to reach. Staying true to form, our last ride spilled us out into a taproom. Scot met us there, then took us around town to all the great beer spots before heading to his house.

As an avid homebrewer himself he had plenty of bottles to share and plenty of gear to geek over. Most critically though, he had his keg of Ryeway at the ready.

We toasted to our handiwork. The chime of our glasses signaled my final session with the jubilant elixir. Every sip was as much a reflection as it was an inspiration.

Ryeway 117 transcended beer. It became a shepherd, a confidant and the well of rapture for its time.

Kegs eventually run dry, however, and some will never be filled quite the same. All that remains are the fluttering memories of the sweet, the bitter and the spicy kicks that saturated the gone-goings of yesterday. Memories have a purpose, and it's handy to have a handful you can catch a buzz off.

IRISH STOUT

As a kid, my parents vacationed through Ireland and returned with a can of Kilkenny beer — a joke on my first name. The dusty souvenir was on my mind as I sat in Kilkenny myself for the first time, gulping down the town's beer with nostalgic satisfaction.

It was my last name, however, that would instigate the most memorable adventures — and national attention — in the country of my ancestors.

With a childhood dream realized, I shifted bars to one promoting some of the newer craft beers that Ireland had to offer.

My backpack rested against my barstool as I got to bantering with the other two customers in the bar. After a few beers, one of them asked me the question that I was procrastinating on asking myself.

"Where are you staying tonight?" he asked.

I'd only arrived a week earlier into Dublin. From there I hiked and camped for several days along the

Wicklow mountains. My only plan hitching into Kilkenny had been drinking my boyhood dream-beer.

"I'm not sure yet," I thought out loud. "I'll probably wind up camping somewhere. I'm hitching down to Cork next, maybe tomorrow."

"I've got a friend who would probably let you camp in his back garden," he responded, "and if that doesn't work then I may know another good place."

We finished our beers and I followed him to his friend Robbie's, who was home with his girlfriend Helena. They invited us in for tea without hesitation.

Within minutes of talking, they offered up their couch to crash on. Day turned to night and tea turned into beer. Then a night on the couch turned into a proposition of touring around the following day.

Robbie walked me around the castle, the old walls running through town, by churches and all along the river that cuts through. We jumped in his car next so he could show me surroundings towns, stone ruins in fields and a hiking trail along a creek.

By the evening we were back in the living room with Helena throwing stories around again. When they asked about my plans for the rest of the country, I mentioned my idea to visit every bar that bore my last name.

"I went to one already," I told them. "There was a Flannery bar in Dublin, but it was kind of a let down," I laughed.

"Oh, I know the one!" said Helena.

"I marched in during the middle of the day and slapped my passport down on the bar," I told them.

I took a sip of beer, shaking my head with a smile as I recounted the story.

"The place was empty besides the bartender and I, and I told her 'I'm a Flannery too!', but she just looked at me like, 'What are you drinking?' No reaction at all."

"Oh no!" Helena laughed.

"So I just said, 'Guinness, I guess.' Then I drank it and left," I said.

"Oh well," I shrugged, taking another sip of beer. "I'll still try to pop into the other ones while I'm looping around the country. Might as well."

Helena had a more ambitious idea.

"You should contact some radio stations, they love these kinds of stories!" she insisted.

I laughed, brushing it off, but she was persistent. Robbie nodded in agreement.

She looked up the contact information for two of the most popular radio shows, all but forcing me to send them emails. I fired off a couple messages and we stayed up a while longer, changing the subject to their treehouse plans and other travel stories.

In the morning they'd gone to work by the time I woke up, now ready to hitchhike to Cork. On my walk out of town, I caught a WiFi signal and paused to check my messages.

I had to blink my eyes open wider when I saw

responses from each of the radio stations. Both had given me phone numbers asking that I get in touch immediately.

An open hostel on the same street let me use their phone. I called the Ray D'Arcy show first — they wanted to get me on the air that same day, even if it meant buying me a train ticket to Dublin.

I called the other station next to find they had the same urgency.

"Great!" I told them. "I just got off the phone with the Ray D'Arcy show as well, they're looking to do the same!"

My excitement was met with discontent. The two stations were in competition, apparently. The woman on the phone told me if I appeared on Ray's show then I couldn't do theirs.

I took the advice from the hostel's front-desk girl and chose the Ray D'Arcy Show.

Rather than going back to Dublin, they said I could do the interview over the phone later that afternoon. When the craft beer bar opened, they were more than willing to let me use their landline for the call.

After a couple pints the phone rang and there I was, live on the radio talking to Ray. He asked about my eight years on the road, hitchhiking, and then focused on how this was my first time in Ireland "chasing my roots" via Flannery bars.

After the segment, they told me to stick around to talk again at the end of the show. By then, several people had called in to mention a Flannery pub in their town — many of which I hadn't known about.

They also reached out to a famous rugby player, Jerry Flannery, who was on the call when we went back on the air. He had his own Flannery pub in Limerick and invited me to drop in.

The flow of attention was surreal.

Limerick seemed to be the Flannery epicenter. Besides Jerry's pub there were five others in and around the city. Altogether, I now had a list of about a dozen Flannery bars to visit throughout the country, where before I'd only been aware of four or five.

After the interview I hiked out of town, back on the track my day began with. I'd contacted a Couchsurfing host in Cork and wanted to make it there before dark. It took seven different rides and bits of walking between each, but I made it.

John was my host — a skinny guy with long, gray hair, originally from Los Angeles. He used to do a fair bit of hitchhiking in his day as well, and still traveled periodically, but was more or less settled in Ireland now.

The next day he said he'd be busy until the evening, so I bounded into the city on my own. I circled the streets, discovered some breweries and got a feel for the downtown. Feeling satisfied, I marched out of the center towards the one Flannery bar in the city.

After the underwhelming experience at the Dublin bar I figured I'd be a little more low key. I ordered my Guinness and kept to myself, glancing around as other chatted away to each other.

Halfway through my pint the bartender started making conversation, so my mission naturally came up anyway.

"My last name is Flannery, actually," I started, without the passport flashing or over-excited tone. "I was thinking I'd visit as many Flannery bars as I can while I'm over here."

"You're the fucker from the radio!" he exclaimed. "That pint is free! We've been waiting for you!"

"Really?" I asked, my excitement now matching his.

"Yes!" he turned to the other guys at the bar. "This is the American from the radio!"

He made a phone call, then turned back to me.

"The owner ordered you a custom, engraved bottle of Jameson. He'll be in tomorrow," he told me.

For several more hours everyone in the bar was rattling stories back and forth with me. Pints of Guinness and glasses of Jameson slid my way faster than I could drink them.

Properly buzzed and feeling the love, I pulled myself away from the bar stool. Despite the wild fun, I had to go meet up with John as we planned.

I joined him and his friends back downtown at their regular pub. After a few drinks his friends dropped out, but John and I were keen to keep going. We poured into the streets looking for the next spot.

"You're too drunk," one bouncer told me calmly. High praise in Ireland.

It was getting late and places were closing down,

but John said he knew about a backdoor to a hostel we could try. The door was open, so we slipped into their still jumping bar.

"You're not gonna fall on your ass again, are you?" said a bartender who spotted John right away.

I don't think John remembered the precise incident the bartender was speaking of, but he wasn't surprised either. The skeptical bartender poured us some drinks anyway. We kept to ourselves around the pool table for several rounds as my memory faded to black.

When I snapped back into consciousness, I was walking through a neighborhood in early daylight. I tried to decipher where I was and how I'd gotten there, and more importantly, how to get to John's place.

Somehow I navigated back, but if he was there, he was asleep and unresponsive. I decided to walk into the city again, stalking around like a zombie. Some food helped the situation, and after a while I looped back to find him now awake.

He, too, had no memory between the billiards table and waking up at home. Some nights are too good to remember.

I made another stop into Flannery's the next day, meeting the owner this time. He kept my glass full, once again, while showing me their expansion plans and talking about my trip.

My next round of Flannery pubs were the half dozen in Limerick. I had no reason to hurry though, and people were telling me I should pass through

Ireland's southwest beforehand.

My first ride in that direction was from a bar owner who'd heard my story on the radio. I hadn't realized it, but when I sent Ray an email — thanking him and telling him about the kicks at Flannery's in Cork — he read it on the air. They'd continue broadcasting my updates all the way along, and more people were starting to notice.

I reached the little town of Killarney, which was a jump off point to the Ring of Kerry. This was the road I'd been told about — a scenic loop in the southwest.

An older man with a scrunched-up, smiling face whipped us around the curves as the beautiful mountainous scenery started to expose itself.

A woman and her daughter gave me a short ride next, overly impressed that I used to be an audio engineer in New York. They assumed I knew every American artist they could name.

Later I got a ride from a guy telling me about some family drama involving a cow. I couldn't follow the story, but it kept me cheerful.

A local guy had passed me twice during the day, and now picked me up on his way to a beach bar up ahead. He invited me to join him for a beer.

I filtered through the bar talking to just about everyone. A French girl was there as a nanny, and the family she was working for bought me a beer as we chatted for a while. Others invited me to smoke a bowl outside. Several had heard the radio show and bought rounds as well, just to hear some more stories.

As the action dwindled, I got a recommendation about a beach I could camp on if I walked down the road a bit. Instead, a pair of passing headlights pulled over. The girl driving knew about an abandoned hotel overlooking the sea, just a few minutes up. I set up my bivy on the cliff there — home for the night.

Rain poured down in the morning as I continued around the great ring road. My first ride was from a lady who stopped to get us coffee, and next I was lifted by a guy who used to work on chimneys in Iranian nuclear facilities.

A trio of drunks livened up the day after that, whisking me with them to a pub up the road.

They bought several pints as the girl tried to string a story together about her morning.

"Muff diving," "Being on the rag," and "Jizz everywhere" she cackled, throwing back beers through her incoherent story.

She had us all cracking up — even funnier for me trying to parse out the details through her thick accent.

I left them there and caught a couple more rides to Dingle — a mix between a fishing and tourist village. I took a lap around before aiming myself at the almighty Limerick.

After four rides, the dipping sun shifted my mindset from cars to camping. A ride came first though — Dennis was celebrating his 52nd birthday and on his way home to Limerick.

Landing in a city center without somewhere to stay isn't the best idea. I had a host set up there, but not until the next night. I kept my eyes to the sides of the road, still scoping out camping options as we got closer.

As we talked, Dennis half-offered to let me stay at his house for the night. He said he'd have to go check with his family though, then maybe come back and get me.

I rolled the dice and fortuitously got dropped off at one of the six Flannery bars in the city where I'd wait for his decision.

It was Jerry Flannery's, the rugby player I'd spoken to on the radio. Unfortunately, the bartender said he'd be out of town for a couple weeks. I sipped my Guinness anyway, and by the end of the pint Dennis had returned with good news.

Back at his house in the hills I chatted with his family over tea for a while, then had a comfy room to myself for the night.

The next day, they dropped me off downtown for a morning of rambling the streets, then I honed in on the largest of the Flannery bars in town.

The bartender poured me a beer as I told him about my mission. In the next room he showed me a showcase full of old Guinness bottles with the Flannery name inscribed. There were also framed news clippings about the bar from over the years. It was the first of the pubs that had a strong connection to the family name.

The owner came down, a Flannery himself,

aware of me from the radio. He had a Flannery T-shirt for me and asked the bartender to pour me a whiskey tasting tray.

At last, I felt like I was in the company of family — a distant cousin, perhaps.

While sipping the whiskies, a beer rep arrived from a craft brewery called White Gypsy; he was there to clean the lines. He poured me free pints of his beer while telling me about the growing craft beer scene in Ireland.

Pat Flannery popped in next — he ran one of the other Flannery pubs in town. That's when I realized that all six of the pubs in town were part of the same extended Flannery family — the family that was now treating me as one of their own.

So, feeling buzzed from the beer, whiskey and good conversation, I meandered on over to Pat's bar. I only had time for a pint there, as by then I was due to link up with my Couchsurfing host, Tanya.

She picked me up with her son and we headed back to her house in the countryside for an early night.

I did some more wandering around downtown the next day, but then it was back to the mission.

Flannery's on Shannon was my first stop. They too had heard me from the radio. They shook my hand, grabbed another Flannery T-shirt and poured me a Flannery-branded stout. A lady Flannery came out with a phone book so I could marvel at the list of Flannery's within it.

An aged Flannery whiskey was pulled out next

from their anniversary, and they generously shared it with me. They took my picture outside the pub and poured me one more stout before I had to keep moving. It felt like a hero's homecoming.

I squeezed in the fifth Flannery's pub for more of the same hospitality before Tanya got off work.

The sixth and final Limerick area pub was outside the city, coincidentally within walking distance of Tanya's countryside home. She dropped me off there on the way back.

I ducked my head inside to the quiet place and met the owners who poured me a pint before showing me around. Outside there were some family gravestones. Inside the walls were also lined with old newspaper clippings about the pub and the family from over the years. My connection to Ireland was getting stronger by the hour.

The next morning Tanya brought me back to town on her way to work. I had my backpack and was ready to move on north from Limerick. There was one last order of business, however.

The radio station had continued reading my updates on the air, and this got the attention of the national newspaper — the *Irish Independent*. They'd sent a photographer to meet me in the city to accompany an interview they wanted to print.

An Irish coffee awaited as I arrived back to the big Flannery's. The photographer snapped my picture by the bar, out front and with the owner. I sipped a couple more pints of Guinness too — for the photos of course.

With my pack full of swag, and my blood coursing with whiskey and Guinness, it was time to keep moving in my clockwise-fashion around the island.

There were just three more Flannery pubs left to visit. Before the next one, in Galway, I'd found a host to stay with on a farm along the way.

I hitched just two rides to get there, walking down some dirt roads until I reached some houses with cows out front.

Tim, about my age, periodically had Couchsurfers and volunteers visiting his family farm. He walked me around the property and showed me the little house I could stay in. We stayed up in the kitchen swigging his homemade nettle wine, rambling on about philosophy and other pertinent nonsensities.

The second day we hopped on his little boat and buzzed through the waterways to a small island, then to the far shore for a pint.

By night, we'd driven his car into town for a long night at a bar before bumping on back to the farm.

With neither of us backing down, he broke out more nettle wine, and vodka when that was finished. We smoked his salvia in the midst as well — transporting me into a chaotic cartoon-scape for a short spell.

In the next room we launched into an unhinged jam session. I wailed away on his drum kit while he howled into a microphone, professing the intricacies of the universe as he saw it.

By the second morning, we realized we'd drive

ourselves to madness if we kept up this pace. It was time for me to meander on back to my Flannery pub hopping.

Before I left, I got a phone call from the reporter at the *Irish Independent*, asking me a series of questions for the interview they were going to publish. This eased me back into a mental state suitable for the rest of the world.

I hitched a short ride first, but my second took me directly to the Cliffs of Moher.

I'd always pictured Ireland's rolling green hills dotted with sheep. The likes of these towering cliffs exposed another level of awe I hadn't considered.

I walked the length of them, all the way to the small town of Doolin where the rain picked up. Light showers were the norm in Ireland, although often they swept in and out.

I stopped for coffee, waiting for it to pass. When I realized it wouldn't, I stepped out to hitch a ride to the next town. I planted myself in front of a pint at a pub there, again waiting for a break in the rain that wouldn't come.

Feeling beaten as it got dark, I gave in to the call of a nearby hostel to get a dry bed for the night.

Inside, I met the generic cast from every hostel experience ever written. The obligatory group of Germans were in my bunk room. An Australian was making new friends. The middle-aged Spanish cyclist was giving unsolicited advice to anyone who'd listen. Two English girls were plotting every detail of their days ahead.

The sunny morning came and I walked my way out of town. A short ride got me to a grocery store where I got the makings of a sandwich, resting for a moment.

Then, a familiar looking group gave me a lift — the German characters from the hostel. They were heading to Dublin, so I didn't ride with them long. A couple heading to Galway was behind them though, and they brought me right to Flannery's Hotel.

This was among the underwhelming. I strode past signs that suggested only hotel guests were allowed at the busy bar. The bartender was indifferent to my story and didn't believe an actual Flannery owned the place. I drank down my pint and hustled towards the action in Galway's center.

I made fast friends at a craft beer bar while ordering glasses of Irish hoppiness. One girl was intrigued by the concept of Couchsurfing, so she came with me when I left to meet them.

We joined them and their friends at another pub in the center. The drinking session launched off through town and spilled back into their house until late.

A slow, hungover day ensued. There was a lethargic exploration of other pubs later, but sleep came much earlier than the night before.

I hitched two rides to Athlone, right in the center of Ireland. The Flannery bar I'd come for wasn't open, and after some peeking in and asking around, I discovered it was closed for the day. This being a Tuesday, was the one day of the week they were shut, said the guys next door.

I'd have to zigzag back later — which turned out to be the better roll.

Besides the postponed Athlone, the only pub that remained was "Flannery Bistro" in Ballinrobe. I hitched a ride back to Galway and two more rides north to get there. Like Flannery's Hotel in Galway, however, it was a bit of a letdown.

A Flannery had owned the place years ago, but different owners took over. It was more of a restaurant than a bar, anyway. I drank my pint all the same, now knowing only the pub in Athlone was left between me and completion of my mission.

Before returning there, and back to Dublin for my flight onto Scotland, I wanted to continue north to round out the island.

I got a sunset ride from a local who showed me a big shed on a property that belonged to his friend.

"You can camp underneath there tonight," he told me. "He's out of town and wouldn't mind anyway. If someone says something just give them my name."

I slept undisturbed, then got myself to the base of Croagh Patrick, a small mountain up the road. A march to the top rewarded me with a view of the greens and blues of the ever awesome landscape.

I started hitching towards Achill island next, a suggestion I'd gotten from several people.

Colin picked me up as I got going, telling me about his farm in the area. He said he had a constant stream of international volunteers helping him and his wife, which was a few younger Germans at the moment. He was a friendly guy, but I didn't think too much of it until a couple rides later.

I ran up to a car that pulled over, squeezing into the back seat. A woman was driving with a younger guy up front and two girls around my age in the back.

They explained — with their German accents — that they were taking the day off from volunteering on the woman's farm to explore the area.

"I think I may have met your husband earlier," I told the woman driving. "Is his name Colin?"

They looked at each other with silly bewilderment as I explained how he'd picked me up earlier in the day.

"What a small world!" Ali, Colin's wife, said. "Do you wanna join us for lunch?"

By the end of lunch I was cemented into the rest of their day's adventuring. We ran their dog along beaches, played by the bay and climbed up peaks overlooking the island.

At the end of it, Ali was telling me about an extra bed in the trailer where the girls were staying. Everyone was all smiles as I stuck with them, heading on home for dinner.

We arrived at the house where Colin was by himself at the kitchen table, glancing up at me in amused perplexity as I walked through the door.

"Remember me?" I laughed.

The serendipitous tone rang through the spirited night around the table and reverberated into breakfast the next morning.

I carried the vibe with me as I returned to the road. The light rain felt refreshing while I lifted my thumb to the passing cars.

It took six rides to get up to Donegal. Dunkineely was the tiny town I was aiming for, and that's all I said to the last guy who picked me up.

"You're going to see Damien," he said with a smile. "I'll take you right to his pub, he's a friend of mine."

Damien and his dad each ran a pub on the short stretch of town. An apartment above one of them used to operate as a hostel, but they discovered Couchsurfing and never looked back.

The nearby sea cliffs, Slieve League, rivaled the Cliff of Moher. Damien drove me out to hike on my own along them the next day. I spent a few days between there and his pub getting to know him and other guests he had coming through.

He loved the company, so much so that he was having a "festival" the coming weekend. He planned to host several dozen people from near and abroad for a few days of music, trips and pub shenanigans.

It didn't take much to talk me into that. In between, I had time to jump over to Northern Ireland and back.

I hitched up to Giant's Causeway — yet another set of stunning sea cliffs — and then over to Belfast.

By Friday afternoon I'd circled back to Donegal where I hiked to the top of Mount Errigal — the highest point in the county. I sloshed down from the clouds to the boggy base where my thumb guided me back to Damien's pub in Dunkineely.

The music jammed on as pints and people kept pouring in. There were girls from Germany, a woman from California, a New Zealander on his first world-trip and plenty more from Ireland and afar. A Canadian girl who arrived later had hitchhiked herself, clear from Cork to there in a single day.

Damien arranged a bus for us the next day to take us around the area. We spent hours hiking the gorgeous sea cliffs, then to waterfalls and other pubs for music.

We spent the night and the next day in similar fashion, bouncing between the two pubs in town and several of us roaring until the sun came up.

On Monday morning, I awoke hazily to the California woman's voice saying it was time to go. My new friend was giving myself and the Canadian girl a ride out of town.

We rolled along in a half-drunk, hungover sort of euphoric, delirium. The green hills waved past us in a vibrant blur. In a few hours we reached Athlone, my stop. They were continuing on, but joined me for one last drink while I waited to meet my host for the night.

As they were leaving the Canadian girl gave me a shy kiss on the cheek. In a rush, the weekend replayed itself as I realized a slew of missed opportunities within. But I snapped into the next dynamic.

My host was a fun-loving designer who lived just a short walk from Flannery's. It happened to be one of her go-to bars, particularly on Mondays, which was blue's night.

That afternoon I met her friends, grabbed dinner and went fishing in the park. As night approached, my excitement was bleeding into all of us. It was time to complete my mission.

"Flannery!" the blonde-haired woman behind the bar shouted as I cracked the pub door open.

Recognizing my face, now that the newspaper had printed my picture, she came running over to give me a vivacious hug.

This was Ann Flannery — surely a distant aunt of some kind. From that moment on, the night sustained a blistering energy.

The local paper was alerted just a few doors down. Ann introduced me to everyone in the pub as if they were also a Flannery, playfully skipping through the crowd.

"This is Paul Flannery, the town banker!" she said.

She rushed me over to the next person.

"This is Tim Flannery, the doctor!" she smiled.

We continued all the way through to the blues band and the Flannery dog in the corner while a reporter snapped photos.

Whiskey filled in the gaps between pints, which I was pouring myself at one point. We raged and howled as the band played on, jabbering deep into the night of celebration.

Despite a wild hangover, we returned the next

day. Somewhere in the night I'd agreed to be filmed for some kind of TV show. Being a Tuesday, the bar was closed, as I'd learned, but Ann opened for the film crew to come in. The "prop" pints went a long way in evening me out.

The cameraman was excited to get a shot of me hitchhiking, as I genuinely needed to get on the road to Dublin before dark. My incarnate homecoming to Ireland had reached its culmination, just in time for a flight to Scotland leaving the very next day.

I shot up in the air towards Glasgow still on a high. Ireland fulfilled my whimsical expectations, but its essence also overflowed into a gregarious, panoramic sublimity that confirmed my connection to the island.

As usual, my onward propulsion was unaffected by how deeply I fell in love with the place, the people or the experience. I belong piercing through the cloud's glow of potential, lifting over the crests of mountain passes and racing the sun to furthering horizons. Onto the next adventure, into the next beer.

Kenny Flannery

Time for a beer run, you've reached the end. Here's some pictures in the meantime:

Amber American

Kenny Flannery

German Schwarzbier

Kenny Flannery

Belgian Quad

Kenny Flannery

Northwestern IPA

Keg Location Clue 4:
To the north a Rainbow is seen in the cold
And to the south the gates arE pearly and bolD.

Kenny Flannery

Ryeway 117

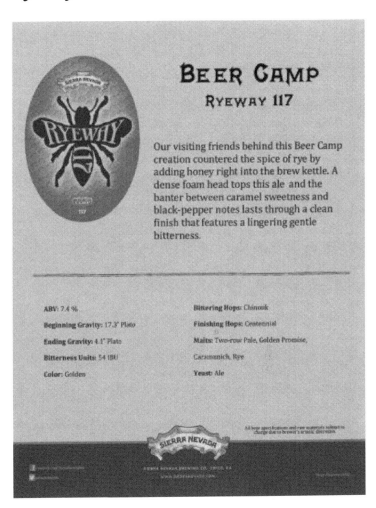

BEER CAMP
RYEWAY 117

Our visiting friends behind this Beer Camp creation countered the spice of rye by adding honey right into the brew kettle. A dense foam head tops this ale and the banter between caramel sweetness and black-pepper notes lasts through a clean finish that features a lingering gentle bitterness.

ABV: 7.4 %

Beginning Gravity: 17.3° Plato

Ending Gravity: 4.1° Plato

Bitterness Units: 54 IBU

Color: Golden

Bittering Hops: Chinook

Finishing Hops: Centennial

Malts: Two-row Pale, Golden Promise,

Caramunich, Rye

Yeast: Ale

All hops specifications and raw materials subject to change due to brewer's artistic discretion

SIERRA NEVADA

SIERRA NEVADA BREWING CO. CHICO, CA
WWW.SIERRANEVADA.COM

Irish Stout

Flannery's bar crawl

Since quitting his high-powered job in New York eight years ago, Kenny Flannery has backpacked around the world. Now in Ireland, he has vowed to visit every pub bearing the Flannery name. Here, he shares a pint with GRAHAM CLIFFORD

About The Author

Kenny Flannery left his apartment in New York City in the summer of 2007, and has been living on the move ever since. As you may know by now, he does a whole lot of hitchhiking while drinking amazing beer along the way.

He hosts "The Freestyle Travel Show," which you can listen to anywhere that podcasts are found.

Stories and advice from the road are also shared regularly at: http://www.hobolifestyle.com

@HoboLifestyle everywhere else.

Thanks...

To my friends and family.
To the hundreds of people who've invited me to stay for a night.
To the thousands of people who've given me a ride.
And the thousands of breweries making great beer.

I'll see you down the road.

Made in the USA
Columbia, SC
29 April 2021

36506242R00076